OUR BEST DAYS

by
Sally Coleman
and
Nancy Hull-Mast

HAZELDEN®

Hazelden
Center City, Minnesota 55012-0176

©1990 by Hazelden Foundation
All rights reserved. Originally published
1990 by Parkside Publishing Corporation
Published by Hazelden 1994
Printed in the United States of America
No portion of this publication may be
reproduced in any manner without the
written permission of the publisher

ISBN 13: 978-1-56838-114-5

This book is lovingly dedicated to our sons:

Tim, Murphy, and Dan Tobin

and

Jack and Tyler Mast

OUR BEST DAYS

ACKNOWLEDGMENTS

We would like to thank Gretchen Douthit and Kristen Ison for the writing they contributed to this book, and Sheelagh McGurn for her careful editing. And, although they are not listed as contributors, we would also like to thank the young people of all ages who read our manuscript and whose encouragement has made its mark on our hearts.

The Authors

As we move through the coming year, it is our wish that you discover, as we have, the sense of adventure and openness and forgiveness that lives in this book. We wish you growth and gratitude, self-love and serenity, and the best day of all—today.

The Editors

*I have a new philosophy. I'm
only going to dread one day at a
time.*

Charles Schulz

Living one day at a time is a big project.
Most of us have just enough faith, patience,
and courage to last 24 hours. We all seem to
be in need of a daily refueling.

Living in today helps keep our lives balanced and simple. At first, we may need to
practice staying in the present. We may find
that we need to keep bringing ourselves back
to today from yesterday or tomorrow.

There is nothing that will happen today
that we can't, with God's help, manage.

*Today let me keep my feet firmly planted in the
bedrock of the present, my only reality.*

*Nothing is so much to be feared
as fear.*

Henry David Thoreau

There are often days when we must do
something we have put off doing, or something we fear. This is normal life, and it
happens to us all. Not every day is like this,
but when one is, we can say a prayer, accept
the fear, and not struggle against it. Being in
recovery means we need to live fully in the
world and do things in spite of fear.

In recovery, we learn that through acceptance and trust, we can do difficult things.
When we fight fears, we usually lose the
battle and actually become more frightened.
Quiet cooperation with God's plan for us won't
always remove fear, but it will make it more
manageable.

*Today let me understand that faith makes
fear manageable.*

*Thinking thoughts doesn't make
us bad and thinking thoughts
doesn't make them happen.*

Allen Smith

Sometimes we get scared by the things we think. We start to worry that our thoughts may become reality. We might believe our thoughts are so strange that no one else could possibly think the same things. As teenagers, we might worry about losing control and killing a loved one. Having thought this once, we can become obsessed with worry about it.

Obsessive thinking can make us sick. We can get help to control obsessive thinking. We also need to remember that many other people have had the same troublesome thoughts and fears and have gotten over them.

Today let me trust that there is nothing I think or do that is too bad to tell someone else.

January 4

*Lost warriors have only to open
their eyes to find the right and
good path.*

Chief Red Mountain

We all carry a fountain of joy inside. This joy is not something special given to only a few of us. An abundance of joy, happiness, and peace is our right. Our hearts were meant to be full of love and laughter.

We have been promised that our lives will get better. Even the worst situations will be made right. As we walk the path of recovery, our lives do get better. When we think we have reached our limit of joy and happiness, something else happens. We get happier! Life will not be without troubles, but joy and gratitude will heal all wounds and shine through all problems.

Today let me accept, without fear, the new joy I feel.

Sometimes when I look at all my children, I say to myself, "Lillian, you should have stayed a virgin."

Lillian Carter

We sometimes feel very far from our parents. Our addiction made us loners, made us believe we didn't need anyone—not even our parents. Now we are beginning again and want to feel the closeness that has been lost. But we may be afraid of their reaction if we tell them how we feel. Will they understand if we try to talk to them about our fears? Can we tell them we love them?

It might be easier to go on the way we have, but our program challenges us to confront our fears and take action in our lives.

It helps to remember that we don't need to do it all at once. Just a kind word or a hug is enough to begin with.

Today let me discuss these problems with my sponsor and look for solutions.

January 6

*We have within us a limitless
supply of new beginnings.*

Joan Fitzgerald

We can start our day over any time we
choose. If we wake up crabby, on the "wrong
side of the bed," we are not doomed to a day of
gloom. Each minute can be a new reality for
us. We can start a new day with just an ounce
of willingness. There are days when we get
stuck in the mud of depression. Part of us
wants to begin again and another part seems
to like to dig around in our problems. We
might even feel like just staying stuck in the
dark side of today. As addicts, we are used to
feeling betrayed, injured, persecuted, and gen-
erally sick and tired.

Willingness to try another way is the
start. We can take a second to choose to look
at our gray day in a more positive way.

*Today let me start over when I find myself
glued to my troubles and negativity.*

*There is no failure except in no
longer trying.*

Elbert Hubbard

If we fail at something it means we took a
risk. If we apply for a job and get turned
down, if we try out for a team and don't make
it—these things tell us we bothered to take a
risk. When we were using, we only risked
what we didn't value—our lives. That requires nothing like the sober courage it takes
to risk so-called failure. So now, when we fail
at something, instead of feeling like a failure,
a part of us can feel like a winner for having
taken the risk in the first place. Now we can
begin to treat ourselves to the small successes
that used to be invisible.

*Today let me be gentle with myself and simply
be willing to try.*

January 8

*The only problems money can
solve are money problems.*

Frank M. Hubbard

Sadly, money in our society is often a
yardstick of how much we can do. We sometimes begin to think money is the most important thing. It takes money to do almost
anything—but not everything.

Ask the parents of a dying child how
important money is. Given a choice of money
or the child's health, they would certainly
take health. Money can buy big cars, jewelry,
homes, and clothes, but it can't buy integrity,
honesty, friendship, or love. Most of all, it
can't buy sobriety. No amount of money can
take the place of our new lives, or buy the
happiness and self-love we are feeling today.

*Today let me do my best to earn the money I
need without believing it has the power to
bring me happiness.*

*He that cannot forgive others
breaks the bridge over which he
must pass himself; for every man
has need to be forgiven.*

Thomas Fuller

Often we're afraid to forgive others who've hurt us because we believe that, in doing so, we are permitting what they've done. This is not true. When we forgive, we are saying "I pardon you, I give up any claim for revenge, you are no longer an enemy."

Relationships are not all black and white. We can forgive people and still not want to spend time with them. Forgiveness is for ourselves. It is a housecleaning of the heart. It feels good to sweep out the resentments and bitterness, lift up the windows, and let in the forgiveness.

Today let me offer forgiveness, either silently or out loud, to someone who has hurt me.

January 10

*To the extent that we want
something from someone, to that
exact degree we will be in pain.*

JoanWalsh Anglund

The more we want from others, the less we seem to get. "I want what I want when I want it!" is a setup for pain. To constantly expect and demand from others is like feeding fat to our egos. They grow spoiled. After a while, we become obsessed with controlling others. Every rejection is magnified by our blaming anger. We feel we have an empty hole inside that must be filled by others.

When we stop expecting, demanding, and controlling, new miracles begin to happen. People actually start to move toward us. We become safe to others as they sense they can freely choose to give or not to give to us.

*Today let me know that what I have been
needing all my life is really inside me.*

*Your position never gives you the
right to command.*

Dag Hammarskjold

The ability to blend power and kindness
is the mark of a compassionate person. As we
begin to get honesty and balance in our lives,
we find that people turn to us for guidance
and leadership. Leadership carries a price
tag of responsibility with it.

We need always to go very carefully when
asked to take on a leadership role. It is wise
to lead with our actions, not our words. When
we do this, we know that no matter what
others do, at least we are moving ourselves.

*Today, let my actions follow Your will and
they will lead others.*

*If you have built castles in the
air, your work need not be lost,
that is where they should be.
Now put foundations under them.*

Henry David Thoreau

Positive thinkers have dreams, set goals,
make plans, follow through on plans, and get
results. *Action* is the magic word. The more
we believe in ourselves, the more we are able
to accomplish.

One way to start getting positive results
in our lives is to watch how others succeed. If
we stick with the winners and learn from
their attitudes, we can do just about anything
we make up our minds to do.

*Today let me choose to set a goal for myself
and follow through until I attain it.*

*The love of our neighbor in all its
fullness simply means being able
to say to him: 'What are you going
through?'*

Simone Weil

Love is listening to our friends and really
hearing what they have to say. Sometimes
we find it hard to listen because we are so full
of ourselves. We don't hear well when we stop
listening and start thinking about our own
responses.

We feel most heard when someone doesn't
try to fix us or give us all the answers. Mostly,
we need a friend to let us pour our hearts out,
to tell our stories to. In giving another the
same attention we'd like to have, we live by
the Golden Rule, and we allow ourselves the
rewards of true friendship.

*Today let me bring a friend my undivided
attention.*

*Who is more foolish, the child
afraid of the dark or the man
afraid of the light?*

Maurice Freehill

We don't have to have a clear picture of
who we're praying to for our prayers to be
answered. Our image of our Higher Power
goes through changes over the years. The
important thing is to believe we're being
heard—to believe that in this world of suffering and joy, there is a greater wisdom than
our own, and that is faith.

Once, we turned to drugs when we felt
empty or confused. Now we can turn to prayer
and meditation. If we doubt whether or not
we're being heard, all we have to do is look
around us at the changes we've made in sobriety and we'll know that, yes, prayers do get
answered!

*Today let me understand that prayer will
work for me.*

*We are better than we know. If
we can be made to see it, perhaps
for the rest of our lives, we will be
unwilling to settle for less.*

Anonymous

We are wonderful, capable human beings
worthy of love and happiness. We all have a
gift to give the world that can't be duplicated.
No one else is exactly like us.

The problem is, we don't believe it. We are
used to thinking about all our negative qualities and become expert at putting ourselves
down. We have a hard time believing and
accepting our own goodness and gifts.

When we have a negative attitude, only
one person can change it—us. We have the
power to choose to change our thinking—if we
want to. It takes a courageous person to risk
getting positive and hopeful. Getting sober is
evidence enough that we have that courage.

Today let me believe I am better than I know.

Success is just a matter of luck.
Ask any failure.

Edmund Wilson

Jim worked very hard all day cleaning cars in a drive-through car wash. He used to have a better job, but he wanted to start a new life so he took what he could get until something better came along. When he got paid, he showed his unemployed brother the check and the brother said, "God, I wish I were you—I'm flat busted! You're so lucky you got some money!"

Often when we're feeling sorry for ourselves, it's because we aren't willing to change the things we can. Jim didn't get money because he was lucky—he got it because he changed himself. He changed his attitude from, "working in a car wash is degrading" to, "I'm proud to take responsibility for myself."

Today let me change the things I can and turn self-pity into self-determination.

*The man who treasures his
friends is usually solid gold
himself.*

        Marjorie Holmes

We are the masters of our own fate! We carry all of the equipment necessary to meet each new challenge but there is also a long rope trailing behind us.

We are the masters of our fate, but we aren't on a solitary journey. The only way we can climb our own mountains is by doing it with others. We learn to be alone by learning to love and trust others. We carry our own lifeline connected to the love and caring of our friends.

Today let me be grateful for my individuality and also for the ties that link me to others.

The beginning of wisdom is to
call things by their right names.

Chinese Proverb

We are getting to know our feelings. At first, they all seem mixed together in two big bags: the good bag and the bad bag. No one taught us how to identify them. Sometimes people tell us we are defensive. They say we should change our reactions. We'd like to, but we have no words to describe or identify our feelings. We can't tell if we're angry, scared, nervous, or sad. Our feelings just feel big and overpowering.

The first step toward changing is to identify the feelings. When we become aware of them, we can choose how to react. When we learn to identify the early bubbles of our simmering anger, we can turn the heat down before the pot boils over.

Today let me identify my feelings.

*At the bottom of most fears will be
found an overactive mind and an
underactive body.*

Dr. Henry Link

Using our heads less and our arms and
legs more in work and play can quiet the
savage beast called fear. Overthink is the soil
that fear grows best in. We become afraid to
risk and make decisions and changes because
we might make a mistake.

How do we get out of our heads and more
fully into life? *Action* is the magic word! In recovery, we are learning to make friends with
ourselves emotionally, spiritually, and physically. We are learning to balance and tune our
lives. Neglecting our bodies and physical
well-being will cause us to be lopsided. We
can find balance through an action as simple
as taking a walk.

Today let me use and appreciate my body.

*Nobody's family can hang out the
sign, "Nothing's the matter here."*

Chinese Proverb

None of us comes from a perfect family,
but if we have any family at all, it's worth the
effort to see what there is to enjoy about it.
Sometimes it's difficult or impossible, because
there's been so much damage. If there's really
nothing left, we have to look for family in the
fellowship of other sober people.

A family is not always people who are
blood related. A family can be people who are
so committed to the growth of each other and
the relationship that they've become brothers
and sisters of a sort. A family is two or more
people who care deeply for one another and
who are comfortable with each other. We can
choose to surround ourselves with others who
we feel this way about.

*Today let me recognize something good in my
family, and work at building a relationship.*

A pessimist is one who burns his bridges before he gets to them.

Sidney Ascher

It would seem that most human beings are quick to be critical. Many of us have become experts at taking the inventories of others. At times, we even seem to get a sense of real satisfaction at judging people and finding their shortcomings. Sooner or later the habit of looking at the world through dark glasses begins to sour our attitude toward life. We become no fun for others to be around.

Negativity is a habit that can be broken with time and patience. The first step is to be aware of our thinking and to make a decision that we want to change. We can begin by training ourselves to look for at least one good thing in every person, place, and situation.

Today let me be willing to look for positives in myself and others.

> *If you have faith as a grain of*
> *mustard seed. . . nothing will be*
> *impossible for you.*

> *Matt. 17:20*

When we repeat the message, "nothing will be impossible for you," we offer ourselves hope and power for the future. We can also change that message to the present tense: nothing *is* impossible.

Recovery has opened the doors and windows of our lives. We are starting to realize that we can be all we want to be. Today, we enjoy the pleasures involved in getting to know a new self. We practice believing in ourselves today. We are full of life and positive energy. Today we know that we are living the adventure of getting to know ourselves and others.

Today let me believe that with the help of my Higher Power, I can achieve all that I dream.

*I feel good about myself since I
started taking care of my body.
It's the home that goes with me
each day of my life.*

Bill L.—Age 17

When we were using, we often neglected
our bodies and personal hygiene. We may
have also stopped getting regular medical
and dental care. It seemed that the ups and
downs of a user's life left us with little energy
for personal care.

Today we are surprised at how much joy
we get out of smelling good and dressing with
care. Many of us are developing our own
personal style.

At first, we might need to force ourselves
to call for regular checkups, but the feeling of
wellness we get from being responsible for our
bodies outweighs our old fears.

*Today let me love myself enough to care about
my physical health and appearance.*

*Recovery can belong to every one
of us. Without exception our lives
can get better.*

Sam Friend

Amy lived for cocaine and partying. The party ended one morning when she woke up and couldn't feel the left side of her body. She was hospitalized and sent to a rehab program.

Amy got sober, but didn't get happy. She felt empty and lost. But, she kept doing the footwork and going to meetings even though she didn't like her new life. In desperation, she decided to attend an AA weekend retreat.

Amy says her life changed that weekend. She isn't sure what happened, but she left the retreat feeling happier than she ever had before. She had a small taste of the joy of recovery that she vowed never to forget. Doing the footwork always pays off.

Today let me keep going until the going gets good.

*People who make the biggest
mistakes are often the holiest.*

Mary Kassan

We've heard it said that it takes a brave person to make a mistake and keep trying. We used to get down on ourselves too much for messing up. We are learning to accept our humanness. It's not such a big deal to be imperfect.

We learn the value of mistakes when we really start to listen to other people. When we sit around and share with others, we find ourselves admiring those people who can admit when they have problems and make mistakes. They really do seem brave to us. They don't seem weak at all. If we keep listening to people being very human, we gradually start to see the light.

Today let me see that it's okay not to have all the answers.

January 26

*Forgiveness is the key to action
and freedom.*

Hannah Arendt

When we refuse to forgive ourselves, we think we are being very noble for not letting ourselves off the hook. What we're really doing, however, is setting ourselves up to use again. We're not accepting the fact that we are powerless over our addiction. It changed us into people who did not act according to our values. We did things that hurt others. If we accept our powerlessness, we are saying that addiction controlled us, and not the other way around. We did not choose this disease and, therefore, must forgive ourselves for getting a human disease called addiction. It doesn't mean our behavior was okay, it means we no longer hold a grudge against ourselves.

Today let me forgive myself.

*I've given up the truth for those
I've tried to please. . . and now it's
my turn.*

Diana Ross

Sacrificing our rights often results in other people mistreating us. We deny our own importance if we say yes when we mean no. Saying no doesn't mean we reject the other person. It simply means we are refusing a request. Some of us become people-pleasers and say yes to everyone and everything. We let other people, places, and things control our lives. We allow our personal freedom to be trampled on. We actually become numb to our own needs.

Learning to say no is an act of love and honesty. When we speak up and are true to our feelings, people know who we are and where we stand.

Today let me learn the healthy art of saying no when it is in my best interest to say it.

*Sometimes a majority simply
means that all the fools are on the
same side.*

Claude McDonald

If we're to stay straight, we have to be
prepared for peer pressure. If anyone tries to
get us to use or do what we know is wrong, we
have to be prepared. Whether we're prepared
to walk away, say "No thanks," avoid slippery
places, or actually tell someone we're recovering, it doesn't matter. What matters most is
knowing in advance what our plan is. If we
are prepared, we'll handle peer pressure well.
Some of us say, "No one pressures me—I don't
have to worry." If we realize there will often
be pressure, we can accept it and be prepared.
The only person who can truly pressure us is
ourself. When we accept this, we have all the
power we need to say no, because we are
saying yes to ourselves.

Today let me know what my plan is.

A thousand eyes, but none with correct vision.

Isacher Hurwitz

William Shakespeare referred to envy as the "green sickness." There are only losers in the game of envy. When we envy someone else, we have judged ourselves and found something lacking.

Lack of self-love is the soil in which envy grows. Envious people are never satisfied. Self-pity is never sitting far from envy. We feel sorry for ourselves for what we don't have. Self-pity is like a swamp, the longer we stand in the muck, the more we stink.

Concentrating on what we do have is the perfect antidote for envy. Every one of us has our own special gifts and talents. We find these by looking at ourselves instead of looking at others. By becoming grateful for what we have, we can rejoice in ourselves.

Today let me be grateful for what I have.

January 30

*Somebody's boring me—I think
it's me.*

Dylan Thomas

Sobriety and recovery are supposed to be fun. Otherwise no one would do it. If we're bored or stagnant, it's because we're not doing recovery right. Recovery is a wonderful adventure filled with new faces, growth, love, acceptance, laughs, peace, serenity, comfort, and fellowship. If we can't find any of that, we need to find out why. Maybe we're purposely trying to avoid the good stuff of sobriety so we can set ourselves up to use again. Or maybe we just need to try some new friends or get involved with a social activity. Today we have the power to take action on our own behalf.

Today don't let me get away with blaming my boredom on somebody or something else.

*If you treat your problems as a
challenge, you can welcome any
disadvantage.*

Charlie Wiedeman

How often do our best plans fall apart? If
we look around us carefully, we'll see we're
not the only ones this happens to. It's important to know that we're not alone, and that
our own will is not often the best way for us.

Nothing happens in God's world by mistake. Each of us can learn and grow from our
problems, no matter how big they are. Sometimes, problems are our best teachers.

Never giving up means being willing to
keep trying to find a solution. In recovery, we
learn to ask the help of our Higher Power and
our friends. We discover the willingness and
strength to find the solution in ourselves.

*Today let me see problems as challenges in-
stead of obstacles.*

February 1

Happiness is not a destination. It is a method of life.

Burton Hillis

The start of a new month is a natural time to take a look at our lives. Are we happy most days? Do we know how to be happy?

We can choose to be happy, no matter what happened in our past or what is going on around us now. But being happy doesn't come naturally to a lot of us. We didn't like ourselves, or our lives, before.

But things are different now. Thanks to our recovery, we are clean and sober and learning to be happy. Being happy starts with the changes in us—being willing to work the steps, to go to any lengths, and deciding to be happy. Today we feel good about ourselves and our lives. We trust that our Higher Power is guiding us to a better life, day by day.

Today help me choose happiness by being grateful for life.

"Thinking," said the little boy, "is when your mouth stays shut and your head keeps talking to itself."

<u>Arkansas Baptist</u>

We need quiet times in order to develop peace and serenity in our lives. We spend most of our days speaking or being spoken to. It's important to set aside time to speak to ourselves. We need to speak to ourselves gently and honestly each day. We need to spend quality time with ourselves to keep in touch with who we are and where we're headed. A diver takes the time for a deep breath and a quiet moment before he jumps, and so it is for us before we jump from one activity to the next. In this way we can honor ourselves and our actions by offering respect for what we've just done, and for what we're about to do.

Today I will have at least one quiet time for myself because I deserve it.

February 3

*There is no height, no depth, that
the spirit of man, guided by a
higher spirit, cannot attain.*

Sir John Hunt

Recovery brings discovery—discovery of
our true selves with all our gifts, dreams, and
visions. Our lives had been in hock, but now
we have the courage to stand on the edge of
endless possibility.

Before, we used to say, "I can't." Today we
find ourselves shouting, "Yes, I can!" Every
new morning that we wake up sober buys a
ride on the joyous train of life. We have a
choice. We are learning to choose joy instead
of pain and hope instead of despair. We are
coming to believe that we deserve to have our
dreams come true.

*Today let me believe that I am full of possibili-
ties, that I can see to the horizon and beyond.*

To be a man is, precisely, to be responsible.

A. de Saint-Exupéry

We can choose to be responsible human beings today. Responsibility used to be a dirty word. Somewhere along the line we seemed to have missed the "responsibility class" in our lives. It is a real experience in living to learn to be responsible. We feel our best at the end of the day when we have given our best efforts to life. We learn to be responsible by doing such little things as wearing a seat belt or doing our homework, talking to a trusted friend each day, promptly saying we're sorry when we have wronged somebody, and working on our sobriety. The more we practice these things, the more we grow.

Today let me list the ways I have learned to be responsible and choose one area to work on.

February 5

*We lie loudest when we lie to
ourselves.*

Eric Hoffer

Addiction helped us become master liars.
We thought we had a lot of power over things
and people. We got this power by lying, frightening people, cheating, and tricking people.
This, though, was the disease at work. Now
we must do the work, not the disease.

Today we can pay close attention to our
motives when we deal with people. We have
the strength of character to stop in the middle
of a manipulation and own up to it. Better yet,
we can recognize when we're about to start
and decide not to. This is called honest effort,
and is the way we live honest lives.

*Today let me see the good in me, to realize I
don't need to resort to dishonesty to get my
needs met.*

*The game of life is not so much in
holding a good hand as playing a
poor hand well.*

H. T. Leslie

We've all had moments when we wanted
to run away and hide from our feelings. In
recovery we don't have that option. We have
to face life. We have to deal with our feelings,
we can't deny them.

All of us face situations that bring up
negative feelings. If a love relationship breaks
up, we'll be hurt. If we do poorly in school or
at work, we may feel cheated. Denying the
feelings only makes them fester inside.

Honestly expressing our feelings is one
way of turning them over to our Higher Power.
As we let them out, He has a chance to
transform them, so they no longer disrupt
our serenity.

*Today let me feel my feelings and turn them
over to my Higher Power.*

February 7

> *Over the years, my brothers and
> sisters have brought out the best
> and the worst in me.*
>
> *Sam Friend*

It sometimes seems that our parents love
our brothers and sisters more than they love
us. Being jealous of a brother or sister is often
a confusing kind of jealousy. One minute we
hate them and the next we love them.

Forgiving seems impossible at times. We
wonder how Mom and Dad can be so nice to
them. We think our parents don't see their
true sides. We may feel like we get blamed for
everything in the family while our brothers
and sisters are praised.

Resentment is often hard to let go of. It is
easier if we remember that we are the only
ones hurt by hanging on to them.

*Today let me be willing to let go of one resent-
ment so I can benefit from a more comfortable
sobriety.*

*I don't know the key to success,
but the key to failure is trying to
please everybody.*

Bill Cosby

"Oh how I wish my dad would get sober."
"Oh how I want my friend to get help with her
eating problem." "Oh how I wish I could make
my mom understand."

When we become obsessed with how we
want others to change, we put our own happiness on hold. As we wait, hoping and schem-
ing about how to get others to see their many
problems, we are neglecting ourselves. It's
almost as if we think it's not fair for us to be
happy when others are miserable. But when
we detach with love, we still care, we still pray
and wish for the best, but we know that other
people's problems belong to them, not to us.

*Today let me accept the fact that if I detach
with love, no one will die from it. I'll just be
more healthy and happy.*

*No man is an island, entire of
itself; every man is a piece of the
continent, a part of the main.*

John Donne

Addiction breeds loneliness. The more
drugs and alcohol we used, the more we isolated ourselves from the things that prevent
loneliness, like real friends, family, hobbies,
and spiritual growth. The more we avoided
these things, the more lonely we felt and the
deeper into our addiction we traveled. Our
friends came in the shape of pills, bottles,
powder, and weed.

Now we are no longer alone. We know the
value of friendship, and we gain and give
support in a group. By offering our attention
to our sober friends instead of our addiction,
we begin to enjoy the fruits of sobriety. Once
again, we are part of the human family.

*Today I will fight off the loneliness by connect-
ing with others who support me.*

*I insist that men shall have the
right to work out their lives in
their own way.*

Giuseppe Garibaldi

It has been said that when we ask someone to do something three times and they
don't, what we're asking becomes our will and
not theirs. Do we really believe that the only
person we can change is ourselves? Is there a
secret place in our hearts that believes we
can, in fact, control others and make them
change? Do we find ourselves hanging on to
the hope that our lives will get better when a
certain person changes and does things our
way?

It is comforting to know that we can't
change anyone but ourselves, and that is all
we need to do. Each time we grow better,
ripples of change go out in all directions.

*Today let me find a positive change I can make
in myself.*

February 11

*One of the roots of the desire for
pleasure is the feeling of emptiness and the pain of boredom
following from it.*

Paul Tillich

We tried to escape pain and boredom, but
found we were worse off than before. Now
we're learning new ways to feel good about
ourselves.

In recovery, we have a chance to find
lasting friendships and a new self-love. We
discover how to share our feelings and get the
help we need to solve problems. As we do this,
we come to understand how much strength it
takes to ask for help.

As we grow in confidence, we find we can
face our feelings honestly. Talking and writing about what's bothering us helps us learn
who we are, and what we need.

*Today let me remember that all the solutions
are within me.*

It's better to know some of the questions than all of the answers.

James Thurber

Recovery is an inner journey, but it often means going outside ourselves. In the past, we often were deaf to the words of others. Now we are discovering that God gave us ears for a reason.

Listening to others may be new to us, but we have so much to gain. Others may have learned ways to solve problems we can't figure out. We may think our lives are unique, only to discover others have had the same experiences. There is so much insight, wisdom, and love to share. Now that we're stronger, we can admit we need help, and accept that help with a joyful heart.

Today let me have the courage to listen to those people whom I respect.

You cannot help men perma-
nently by doing for them what
they could and should do for
themselves.

Abraham Lincoln

Sometimes we feel dependent on what someone says or doesn't say. We have a good day or a bad day depending on another person's behavior. Sometimes we're afraid to be without a boyfriend or girlfriend because we depend on them. Sometimes we're afraid of leaving home because our parents are so convenient.

Dependence isn't always bad. We depend on the Twelve Steps to stay sober and that's good. Today, we can depend on ourselves to ask for help when we need it, and we can depend on our Higher Power to provide us with what we need.

Today let me depend on my Higher Power for support and guidance.

*The moment one definitely com-
mits one's self, then providence
moves too.*

W. H. Murray

We believe God is always with us, but we
can experience His presence more visibly when
we have the courage to act.

Decisions are difficult for us. Sometimes
we won't make a decision until we feel it is
absolutely right. We are finding out though,
that there is some right and some wrong in
every decision. We may never feel completely
sure of anything.

Today, we can risk moving forward and
trust ourselves, with the guidance of our
Higher Power, to move in a right and orderly
direction. Once we start moving, we will feel
better. We usually get what we need when we
begin a course of action.

Today let me stop waiting and take action.

*A problem well stated is a prob-
lem half solved.*

> *Charles F. Kettering*

Denial never really goes away, it creeps
into everyone's life. We may admit we're
powerless over alcohol and drugs but still
believe it was the school's fault that we were
suspended. Denial is especially dangerous
for us, because it spreads, gets out of control,
and eventually takes away our most prized
possession: sobriety.

But now we have the tools we need to
combat denial. Other people can help us see
what we're really doing. We can get to know
ourselves better. And we can learn to change.
Day by day, we grow stronger in recovery.

*Today let me recognize denial, admit what's
wrong, and begin to fix it.*

*Let us not go over the old ground,
let us rather prepare for what is
to come.*

Marcus Tullius Cicero

Sometimes we hang on to the oddest things. For instance, many of us go to a lot of trouble to hang on to old guilt, old mistakes, old loneliness, old hurts, old crimes. We fight like crazy to keep these little darlings near and dear. If we make a mistake, we feel we don't deserve to let go of the self-punishment.

The healthy and sober thing to do is let go of the past. We can cut the chains and shackles of the past that keep us from moving forward. When we cut even one link of that chain, we begin to move more freely toward health and self-love.

Today let me understand that I'm not helping anyone by holding on to the past.

February 17

*Honesty is the first chapter of the
book of wisdom.*

Thomas Jefferson

Denial is something that comes easily to
us. We lied to ourselves about what was happening in our lives. Now, in recovery, being
honest with ourselves is still a tricky matter.
We don't like to admit when we are mean, or
when we are not living up to responsibilities.

When we were in denial, we ran away
from life, we got deeper into our addiction,
and we got into more and more trouble. The
same thing can happen again if we aren't
honest with ourselves. If we deny things, we
will get more and more confused.

But there is a simple answer if we find
this happening to us. We can practice rigor-
ous honesty, first with ourselves, then with
others. It may not be easy to look at ourselves
honestly, but it's essential to staying sober.

Today let me be honest with myself.

*If you always do what you've
always done, you'll always get
what you've always gotten.*

Jessie Potter

When we have to make a decision, we
need to know if we're deciding for ourselves or
to please others. We need to really consider
all our options and not let fear or low self-
esteem force us into a decision we may regret.

We can make a list of our options and the
possible consequences of each and check it out
with someone we admire and respect. No one
can live without support from others. At the
same time, no one can live our lives for us. We
are free to ask for help, free to change ourselves as we choose, and free to enjoy the
rewards.

*Today let me try to make decisions based on
facts and then get a second opinion.*

February 19

No person was ever honored for
what he received. Honor has been
the reward for what he gave.

Calvin Coolidge

There's really only one way to achieve self-respect and that is to act respectably. We can't go back and undo our past. But we can act and behave respectably today, so that when we close our eyes tonight to go to sleep, we can say we have self-respect. A day at a time or an hour at a time, it's our actions now that count. If we put our self-respect on hold, saying something like "I'll have self-respect when I graduate," or "I'll have self-respect when I get a good job," we are putting off what we should do today. But when we live in the present, knowing it's all we have, we can give our best effort to life today.

Today let me treat myself and all those I encounter with respect.

*If you kicked the person who
caused most of your problems, it
would be difficult to sit down.*

Homer Adams

There is a tale about a cowboy who had a
"burr under his saddle." He was always
blaming other people, places, and things for
his woes. For example, if it had rained, the
crop would have been better and he would
have money. If his parents hadn't been so
ugly, he would be handsome and folks would
like him. He didn't realize that the crops were
poor because he planted late, and people would
like him if his attitude was better.

We can make an effort to look to ourselves
when things don't seem to be going well. Our
lives are in our hands, and with the help of our
Higher Power we can smooth them out.

*Today let me realize that, since most of my
troubles are of my own making, I have the
power to solve them.*

February 21

*Advice is like snow; the softer it
falls the longer it dwells upon,
and the deeper it sinks into the
mind.*

Samuel T. Coleridge

Once, we thought we knew everything
and no one could teach us very much. Now we
know others have help and experience and
wisdom to offer us, if only we're willing to
listen. Learning to listen can be hard, especially if we come from a family that didn't
respect each other. But we can learn from
watching others, and talking with other people
about accepting criticism. We're learning new
ways to act and react, and learning to listen is
a good place to start. And in time, maybe
others, even our families, will follow our
example and learn to listen, too.

*Today let me have the right words to share
what is really in my heart.*

There are two tragedies to life.
One is not to get your heart's
desire. The other is to get it.

George Bernard Shaw

Staying clean and sober is often a balancing act. We often don't seem to handle extremes in feelings very well. When we let ourselves get high on excitement or low on depression, we have trouble.

Balance sometimes seems boring. It's hard for us to adjust to a slower pace. Sometimes we even pick arguments just to feel a surge of emotion. It can be helpful for us to remember H.A.L.T. each day. When we feel ourselves getting off balance—too high or too low—we can check and see if we're too hungry, too angry, too lonely, or too tired.

Today let me be open to how I feel.

Dust on diamonds, tears we cry,
first we walk, then we fly.

Mark Chapple

"First things first," "Easy does it," and "Keep it simple" are the touchstones of our recovery. At first, we may grasp recovery like a drowning person. We find that the harder we hold on to our life raft, the harder it is to relax and stay afloat. Letting go a little, we begin to trust that we won't sink. We learn to keep it simple and concentrate on only one thing at a time. We surrender to our life raft and trust that we will be gently carried ashore.

Keeping it simple means trusting others to help us. It allows us to step out of the center of the universe and hold on gently to our supportive friends and our own process of growth.

Today let me get back to basics. Keeping it simple will keep me on the right track.

*I am an old man and have known
a great many troubles, but most
of them never happened.*

Mark Twain

If we spend today worrying about tomorrow or moaning over the past, we'll miss the moment. If we do this every day, we'll miss our lives. We all have regrets from the past and hopes for the future, but they need not interfere with today. What happens to us might not suit our schedule, life might not happen according to our timetable, but then again, how often has our way worked before anyway? Sometimes after something happens for the better, we're glad it didn't happen our way. Our need for today is to live well, with self-love and openness, and to take at least one step forward in our lives.

Today let me concentrate on these 24 hours only.

I am defeated, and know it, if I meet any human being from whom I find myself unable to learn.

George Herbert Palmer

Why do we hate it when someone tells us what to do? Why is it we sometimes can't stand it when someone tries to guide us or educate us? Do we think the person is judging us? If a teacher or boss comments on our work, we need to remember that they are commenting on our work—not on us. If we're asked to clear the table, it's no more than a request for help.

When we are truly sober, we have nothing to hide and no reason to resent. When we are humble, we can feel powerful enough to follow instructions and accept help. When we can accept help, we are humble.

Today let me accept direction from people so that I am better able to offer direction later on.

*There's too much confusion here, I
can't get no relief.*

Bob Dylan

Addiction is like the maze in a carnival
fun house—no matter which way we turn, we
seem to run into blank walls. We used to run
from our problems. We didn't take the time to
reason things through and look for solutions.
We escaped and hoped our problems would
take care of themselves. They didn't.

What can we do when we are lost in the
maze of our own pain? Ask for help.

If the first person we ask doesn't hear us,
we need to keep asking. We then need to take
the next step which is to accept the help we're
given.

Holding the hand of another human being
is the way out of our maze.

*Today let me not be too proud to reach out
when I'm hurting.*

February 27

*That it will never come again is
what makes life so sweet.*

Emily Dickinson

When we were using, we were often impulsive, doing things on the spur of the moment that were harmful to us. We drank and did drugs, we drove recklessly.

Now that we are in recovery, we are learning to curb those impulses. We are learning to think first so we don't do things that put us and others in danger.

In recovery, we learn to do things on the spur of the moment again. We learn to be spontaneous. To be spontaneous is to be natural. As we trust ourselves more, we learn to be natural around people. If we feel like crying, we cry. If we're happy, we laugh. Being spontaneous is like being a little kid again, and it doesn't hurt us or others.

Today let me express my feelings without shame.

*If you're dog-tired at night, it may
be because you growled all day.*

<u>War Cry</u>

Negative attitudes wear us out. Assuming the worst will happen, focusing on just our faults, constant complaining, are attitudes that bring us down. If we stumble on a flight of stairs at school and feel embarrassed, it's going to feel even worse if we growl and curse. We'll feel much better if we laugh at ourselves and see the humor. People want to be around those who are cheerful. The good cheer we send out will come back to us from others who are healthy. We can choose these cheerful people as our friends, and our happiness will grow and blossom in this good soil.

Today let me try to say something cheerful to another.

February 29

*. . . human beings, by changing
the inner attitudes of their minds
can change the outer aspect of
their lives.*

William James

"It's no use, I'll screw it up anyway." This
is an attitude. Some attitudes sound like this:
"I'm great and people should try to please
me," or, "I deserve good breaks," or, "Rules
and laws are for others, but not for me."

Some attitudes can wreck our sobriety,
families, jobs, education, love life, financial
well-being, and spiritual growth. The good
news is attitudes can change. It takes practice but, if we really decide to pay attention
and change the ones that are harmful to us,
we can succeed. In this way we guide our own
growth and create a better, more positive
world for ourselves.

*Today let me pay very close attention to my
attitudes and change the harmful ones.*

I have the tools to survive . . . .

Virginia Satir

Inside us we have everything we need to survive and be happy in the world. Today, we believe our dreams can come true.

A few years ago we didn't have any hope. We felt worthless inside. We looked out of our lonely shell at other people and felt like a stranger in our own world. We were so full of rage and hurt that we wanted to die.

By the grace of God, we finally have begun to walk the long road back. We learned we had an illness. We learned that by being chemically free, one day at a time, we could begin to really live for the first time. We are now learning each day that we are special human beings who have many gifts to give, that we are lovable, capable, and loving.

Today let me use the tools of recovery to survive. My dreams are really coming true.

March 2

*The more a person is at peace
with herself—the less she'll feel
jealous and the more she'll feel
blessed.*

Anonymous

If we get jealous, we need to beware. If
something good happens to a friend, we can
feel glad. It takes nothing away from us. If
someone tells us good news, we might feel a
little jealous, but deep down we're happy for
them and glad they were so lucky. So the
jealousy is just a passing little annoyance to
work on. It tells us we need to believe in
ourselves more so we don't feel threatened by
anothers' good fortune.

If another person deserves good fortune,
so do we, so we can rejoice in their good
news—it only reaffirms our hopes for ourselves.

*Today let me take a jealousy inventory, and
honestly examine why I feel jealous.*

The door to love is only unlocked
for those willing to take risks.

T. Spencer

Asking someone to go out on a date seems impossibly hard to many of us. No one taught us social skills and the ABC's of male-female relationships. Just the thought of calling or talking to someone special makes our hearts pound and gives us a lightheaded feeling. All our worst fears emerge.

These fears are felt by most girls and guys when they begin dating. An important part of our growing up is learning to face the anxiety of exposed feelings in a state of sobriety. Only by confronting and facing our fears can we grow. Dating relationships are a risk at any age, but we have survived worse. We can take heart in knowing that things get easier each time we try again.

Today let me accept the risk in relationships.

The smallest seed of faith is better than the largest fruit of happiness.

Henry David Thoreau

Life crises seem terrifying and endless when they are happening. As we reflect on these stressful periods, we begin to realize that they provide a chance for change and growth. We get a feeling of hope when we think back to past problems that seemed like mountains of despair at the time. Today, many of our mountains of fear are behind us. We have been able to climb these mountains in our lives even though we may have had to take different paths than we had planned.

Now we know that, with faith, we can meet every challenge, that we are given no obstacle we can't turn into an opportunity.

Today let me be willing to let my Higher Power lead me in an orderly direction.

*Mirror, mirror on the wall, who is
the fairest of them all?*

The Wicked Queen

"Ugly, ugly!" This is often what we think
as we look in the mirror. There are days when
we feel ugly no matter how we comb our hair
or wear our clothes. There are days when we
feel like mistakes dressing up as people.

Criticizing ourselves on the outside is
usually caused by the way we feel inside.
When we measure ourselves by our physical
appearance, we will always feel let down. No
one can always be the fairest of them all.

Slowly we are beginning to understand
how our real glow comes from the inside. We
are meeting people in recovery who aren't
beauty contest winners on the outside but
who shine because of their personalities and
their positive energy.

*Today let me accept myself as a lovely person,
inside and out.*

March 6

*Humility is keeping your eyes off
other people's faults, and fixing
them on your own.*

S. A. Rodriques

One of the reasons we judge others is
because we are afraid of being judged. Humility has often been described as the ability to
see our own reality honestly and objectively.
Humility is owning our negative and positive
qualities.

Only humble people have the objectivity,
self-love, and courage to say what is good and
worthwhile about themselves. Humility is
balance. Humility is self-love and the self-
acceptance and willingness to see the shadows and rainbows in ourselves.

*Today let me accept and share my whole self,
believing I am exactly as I'm supposed to be.*

*Experience is the extract of
suffering.*

Arthur Helps

Babies have temper tantrums not only
because they don't know how to communicate
in a more mature manner, but because it's a
way to work out anger. We can do this in a
more controlled way.

When we have been disappointed, we can
say how we feel. That will help. We can also
wait until we are alone and throw a temper
tantrum. We can shout, scream, and pound
the pillows. Doing this is harmless and it feels
good to get the anger out in a harmless physical way without hurting ourselves or anyone
else. By doing this, we perform an act of self-
acceptance, and by releasing the anger, we let
in a balancing calm.

*Today let me get rid of my anger in a physical
way, as long as I do it safely.*

*Out of suffering have emerged the
strongest souls; the most massive
characters are seared with scars.*

E. H. Chapin

When we lose something we value, we
grieve. The more we valued it, the more we'll
grieve. Grieving is natural and desirable. If
alcohol and drugs numbed our feelings, we
probably did not grieve the losses in our lives.

In recovery, all the feelings of loss can
flood back to us unannounced, often with
great force. This is normal, it's important to
feel again, the bad feelings as well as the good.
It's almost impossible, however, to work
through these feelings alone. With the advice
of a friend, another recovering person, or
counselor, we not only come to know ourselves better, but share ourselves with another.

*Today let me find support and fellowship to
help me work through my grief.*

To get courage, you must want it.
When you finally have it, it will
stand between you and all future
adversity.

Dr. Claire Weeks

When we were using, it was easy to think the whole world was against us. We know that's not true today, but it's still easy to slip into self-pity and not have the courage to look at things as they really are.

Luckily, though, we have friends to help us with this. They care enough to help us honestly confront our self-pity. They can help us to look at our own behavior courageously and find the real basis of our problems. Even if we are not the cause of our problems, we can learn to accept life as it comes and have the courage to deal with it sober. With our new selves, our friends, and our Higher Power we can be brave and take on what life has to offer.

Today let me have the courage to be honest.

March 10

*Hope is the feeling you have that
the feeling you have isn't perma-
nent.*

Jean Kerr

When we feel hopeless, it's usually because we've forgotten we're not alone. We've
forgotten there is a Power greater than ourselves that we can call on to fill an empty
heart with good, warm feelings. There is
hope. No one is so bad or worthless that their
life is hopeless. Everyone is lovable and can
feel better. We can call upon our Higher
Power to help turn our discouragement into
hope. When we do this simple thing, we have
already begun to take hopeful action.

*Today let me be courageous enough to look for
hope.*

The sun will set without thy assistance.

The Talmud

Sometimes when we decide to "Let go and let God" we really mean we're going to "Let go and let God with a little help from me." We see a friend in an unhealthy relationship and we feel it's our job to make him see the light. We see a parent has an alcohol problem and we want to make him or her sober. Once we've stated our opinion and told them how we feel, we must let go. If we hang on to the control, we are playing God. We begin to control because we care, but the end result is that our own sobriety slides and falls right into the pit with the one we're trying to save. God gives the gift of sobriety to those who wish to accept it, without our help.

Today let me remember that the only life I can live well is my own.

Human life has its laws, one of which is—we must use things and love people.

Fr. John Powell

Before recovery, we found ourselves loving things and using people. Life was mixed up for us. Chemicals caused us to do cruel things to others. It seems like the longer we are sober, the more we remember our past actions. We feel shame, fear, and helplessness. Thinking about making amends makes us cringe. Some days we want to forget the past and pretend it never happened, but we can't seem to get the door shut tight enough.

Making amends is an act of trust in our Higher Power. Life is sad at times. Some things will never be right. Our job is to make plans, do the footwork, then wait and leave the results to our Higher Power.

Today let me be willing to make direct amends to those I have harmed, whenever possible.

*Gratitude is the fairest blossom
which springs from the soul.*

Henry Ward Beecher

Being grateful is one of the nicest things
we can do for ourselves. If we are having an
off day, or slipping into a little self-pity, it's
amazing what happens when we remember to
be grateful.

The thing we can be most thankful for is
being alive. That's pretty basic, but there are
a lot of addicts who lost life itself. We can also
be thankful for our recovery and the ability it
gives us to live a happy, productive life.

We can be grateful for the support we
have gotten from family and friends. They
cared about us and wanted us to get well. We
can also be grateful for new friends, new
activities, and new ways to have fun. Sobriety
gives us hundreds of things to be grateful for.

*Today let me keep in mind the things I can be
grateful for.*

March 14

I hope I shall possess firmness
and virtue enough to maintain
what I consider the most enviable
of all titles, the character of an
honest man.

George Washington

Being really honest with ourselves and
others requires balance. We have to balance
what our true faults are with our true
strengths. But admitting our faults shouldn't
be an excuse to beat up on ourselves by only
acknowledging our bad points. We need to see
the truth, the good as well as the not-so-good,
our strengths as well as our weaknesses. As
we do this, we can begin to find and love
ourselves as complete human beings. We can
give up the black-and-white way we used to
live and accept our whole selves.

Today let me see all the sides that make up me,
the whole picture—good and bad.

*Wise sayings often fall on barren
ground, but a kind word is never
thrown away.*

Sir Arthur Helps

Making amends to those we've harmed is scary. Part of the reason it's scary is we don't know how the other person will react. Apologizing is kind and courteous to the other person, but the reason we do it is to unburden ourselves from the weight of all that unfinished business so we can get on with our lives. The other person may be glad to hear our amends, or may take it as an opportunity to unleash a lot of anger at us. That doesn't matter. What matters is how honestly we make the amends and how much lighter we feel afterwards.

Today let me strive to make honest amends.

> *Humility is to make a right*
> *estimate of one's self.*
>
> *Charles H. Spurgeon*

Today we are grateful that we don't have to have all the answers. We used to pretend that we knew more than we really did. We felt we had to have an answer to almost everything. We are learning to take a step back from center stage. We can feel comfortable being honest and saying, "I don't know." We feel good about this progress in our recovery.

Today we enjoy being ourselves—not-so-perfect people who are continuing to learn. We are a lot less afraid to get up in the mornings these days. Now we accept our limitations and want to continue to have the courage to be open to learning.

Today let me have more questions than I have answers.

*Some people come into our lives
and quickly go. Some stay for
awhile, leaving footprints on our
hearts—and we are never the
same.*

       Flavia Weedn

There are a few special people in our lives
who we will never forget. Often the qualities
we remember about these people are honesty
and kindness. We like it when someone is
honest with us, and we remember that truth
in our hearts.

It helps to remember the good things
people have said to us over the years—to
make a list of the things we remember—and
hold them inside us.

*Today let me be a person who looks deep into
others and learns to respect their insecurities.*

*The man who has no inner life is
the slave of his surroundings.*

Henri Frederic Amiel

If we cling to the notion that we are all-powerful and all-knowing we may think we are being responsible adults. But really we are being arrogant. We are saying that we, as individuals, are more knowledgeable and powerful than the millions of sober people who have shared their recovery over the years. We are saying that we are wiser than the accumulated wisdom of all the people who came before us. We are saying we are the higher power. Now, if we look back on our lives we can see that this is ridiculous!

How lucky we are now to have friends who help bring us down to earth and a Higher Power to help us soar in our new lives.

Today let me have faith in a Higher Power who will help me and guide me toward greater understanding.

*To have a quiet mind is to possess
one's mind wholly; to have a calm
spirit is to possess one's self.*

Hamilton Mable

One thing we learn in recovery is that we need quiet time every day, time to pray and meditate, time to reflect. But we are so used to going all the time that we sometimes forget to take this time for ourselves. Then we get tired and irritable and lose our serenity.

Our quiet time can take a lot of different forms. It might be time to sit thinking about how much better life is than it used to be. It might be time to read a book, or to pray.

However we relax, it is important that we do it. And it is important that we often use the time to reflect on our recovery and our progress. When we do, we are honoring our selves and our needs and limitations, and we are also rewarding ourselves for work well done.

Today let me take some quiet time for myself.

March 20

Depend on the rabbit's foot if you will, but remember it didn't work for the rabbit!

R. E. Shay

The Twelve Steps work. We know they work, we've seen them work. We've heard and felt them work. But some of us still try to change or alter the Steps. We try to negotiate with the requirements for sobriety. We may feel we have to have the last word. We'll say "I'll do this, but only if. . ." and we put a condition on it. Here is the program that works. It's a gift —let's just grab it. Let's not question, bargain, or negotiate. Let's just take it and run with it.

Today let me remember that the program works—period.

*The hardest thing about trust is
that you need to trust to begin to
trust.*

Sam Friend

The bricks under the foundation of recovery are mortared together with trust. It is a risk to trust someone when they tell us our lives will get better if we follow a few simple steps. Our lives have been filled by self-will and it takes an act of courage to say, "My way didn't work, so I think I'll try yours." Our pain brought us to our knees and we were given the grace to admit we needed help. We began the trust walk we have been on ever since.

Now we are better able to recognize our egos when they get out of control. Each day is a new day as we ask for the grace and willingness to pick up where we left off and trust that our lives will get better.

Today let me have the courage to talk with other people trustfully.

March 22

We need courage to meet what comes and know that whatever it is, it will not last forever.

Leo F. Buscaglia

Sometimes when we see someone who did something great, we think they must have greater wisdom than we, or inside connections, or better luck. Usually the only thing they have that we don't is endurance. People with emotional endurance know, "This too, shall pass." They may have had to make sacrifices like studying when they would rather be sleeping, or taking orders when they would rather be giving them. But they know that the uncomfortable feelings and struggle will give way to a goal reached. The rewards of achieving a goal are self-respect, confidence, and the talent we may have gained that got us there. These things last forever.

Today let me remember that all pain, all negatives, and all difficulties will pass.

*If we wait for the right time to cry
and the right reason to cry, we'll
drown inside.*

Sam Friend

Crying is not an emotional breakdown,
it's an emotional breakthrough. Sometimes
we feel it's weak to cry. We started off with a
whole range of feelings that we showed easily.

But somehow, we learned we shouldn't
have feelings like sadness or anger. We thought
we should always be smiling and happy.

Just as a piano needs all its keys to make
music, we need all our feelings to be complete
and whole. Laughter is a natural reaction to
something funny, tears are a natural reaction
to something sad. We may feel grief over how
much our addiction has cost us, and we can
feel the freedom to cry about it. We're never
too old to laugh or cry.

*Today let me not judge any of my feelings or
hold back from getting to know the real me.*

Success is a journey, not a destination.

Ben Sweetland

Sometimes we work hard to succeed at something and then when we finally get what we worked for we ask, "Is that all there is?" We feel unsatisfied. We've been so accustomed to getting our praise and self-worth from the outside that we were stingy about giving ourselves a pat on the back. Sometimes we look outside for something that's been within us all along.

Now, we can look honestly at our accomplishments and be proud of ourselves for what we do. We can pat our own backs now. We don't have to wait for someone else to do it for us.

Today let me be good to myself and congratulate myself for my small and large successes.

*The world is charged with the
grandeur of God.*

Gerard Manley Hopkins

Trust doesn't come easily for most of us.
We didn't trust anyone—not friends, not
family, especially not ourselves.

Then we began to recover. We were told
to trust other people and to trust a Power
greater than ourselves, a Power we couldn't
even see. People said this Power could restore
us to sanity and keep us sober, if we turned
over our wills and our lives. That was hard for
most of us.

A Power greater than ourselves has always taken care of a lot of things in our lives.
We couldn't make the trees grow, the flowers
bloom, or the seasons change. We couldn't
make ourselves sober. But, with the help of
our Higher Power we are sober today, and we
know we can trust.

Today help me trust my Higher Power.

*Solitude is different than loneli-
ness. It is different than isolation. It is where we meet God.*

Mary Jones

We find God in solitude. Solitude is different than loneliness. It can feel terrible to be
lonely. When we are lonely, our hearts feel
empty and we start to feel that no one really
knows us. Loneliness can make us heartsick.
Solitude heals our hearts.

Solitude is choosing to be alone in order to
make friends with our Higher Power. In
solitude, we feel aloneness—but it is welcome. Only by quieting down the noise of our
lives can we hear and feel God's love for us.

A man once said that after years of study
he only uses one meditation in his quiet times.
He quietly sits and imagines how much God
loves him.

*Today let me trust God enough to spend time
thinking about how much He loves me.*

Guilt: the gift that keeps on giving.

Irma Bombeck

Guilt can serve a useful purpose. It can be a signal that tells us we're not acting according to our values. If we copy a friend's homework and feel guilty, it tells us we're not living up to our values that say cheating is wrong. Guilt can help us correct our behavior.

Now that we're thinking more clearly, guilt can tell us how to live a better life. When we do something that doesn't feel right, we can make a promise to ourselves to do better next time. We can love ourselves for trying to do better, and forgive ourselves for not being perfect today. With the help of guilt, we can learn about our real values, and begin to live the life we once only dreamed about.

Today let me pay attention when I feel guilty and if I'm not living according to my values, make the necessary corrections.

You and I must keep from shame.

A. E. Housman

Shame can make us feel empty inside. Addiction seemed to fill the empty hole in our guts. If we could drink, drug, eat, love, gamble, and run fast enough we thought we might escape ourselves, but it didn't work.

Shame cries to be healed. The empty places inside us cry out for love. Safe, accepting people make a bridge from us to God. Our Higher Power is the love that can reach our deepest empty places. We can begin to feel this love by picking a safe person and sharing something we're ashamed of about ourselves.

Today let me trust the safe people in my life to help me believe that I am not a mistake.

*There can be no rainbow without
a cloud and a storm.*

J. H. Vincent

We all have down days. Some of us thought that once we began to recover, we wouldn't have them any more. But we do. They're not as bad as they were when we were using, but they're still there. The confusing part is that sometimes we know why we're feeling down, and sometimes we don't.

Now we have tools to deal with those days. We can find a friend to talk to. Maybe we were just feeling a little lonely. Are we feeling sad about something? Life holds many losses and events to bring grief.

Whatever the cause, we can be grateful we are in recovery. We know that as long as we stay sober, we'll start feeling betting soon. And we will really appreciate how good we feel then.

Today let me see the rainbow after the storm.

*You may be deceived if you trust
too much, but you will live in
torment if you don't trust enough.*

Frank Crane

Sexual abuse can be devastating. We may be afraid to talk about it for fear others will reject us. We may feel we should have been able to prevent it, or that we should have fought harder to stop it. But if we can take the risk, we find other people understand. It's hard to talk about it the first time, but it gets easier. If we can share our painful secrets, our pain is shared, too, and fades in time.

The way out of the woods of fear is to follow the sun and walk out. We can risk and trust in the power of honesty. When we share the dark, secret places with safe people, we begin to heal in the light of the sun.

Today let me show trust and share my most painful secrets.

*It costs more to revenge than to
bear with injuries.*

Thomas Wilson

One of the things we have to do, if we want
to stay sober and happy, is accept people.
That means accepting everyone, whether we
like them or not. It means accepting all the
members of our family, and everyone else we
have to deal with. If we carry resentments or
grudges against people, we only hurt ourselves. We feel agitated and angry; we get
stuck in self-pity; we stay isolated and lonely.
And we're in danger of relapse.

When we stop judging others and accept
them for who they are, we can have good
relationships. In learning to accept others as
they are, we can begin to forgive our own
imperfections, too. Accepting and loving ourselves and others can bring us peace and
serenity in recovery and in our lives.

Today help me accept people as they are.

April 1

*When people don't forgive, they
probably shorten their lives.*

Doris Donnelly

Sometimes forgiveness seems impossible
and we feel stuck in the quicksand of our own
resentment. When everything else fails, we
can try the "First Five People Forgiveness
Plan." Each morning we make a decision to
forgive the first five people we come in contact
with who make us mad. We forgive all five
people without analyzing or deciding if they
deserve to be forgiven. We promptly forgive
each one of them without exception.

This simple plan can work wonders for
those of us who usually hold on to resentments and anger. Letting go of anger and
resentment lets us feel our loving side. In
learning to forgive others we can begin learning about how to forgive ourselves, too.

*Today let me also remember that I, too, deserve
forgiveness.*

*True friendship is like sound
health, the value of it is seldom
known until it is lost.*

Charles Caleb Colten

Our recovery depends on other people. In order to get well, we have to admit that alone we are powerless over our disease. We need other people to help us. This is a hard thing for a lot of us to accept. We aren't used to needing anyone or asking for help. We all pushed people away after we started using.

In recovery we change that. We are starting a new life based on people helping each other. We are willing to take direction from other people. It takes courage to admit we need help. And it takes humility to ask for help. But now we have friends to help us, a new family to love us and support us. We aren't alone any more.

Today help me reach out to others for what I need.

April 3

*There is a difference between
loneliness and being alone; there
is a choice of mind in being alone;
but loneliness comes up through
the heart into the throat.*

William Faulkner

Loneliness eats us up inside. It is a pain
that runs down the very center of our bodies.
When we were using, we cut ourselves off
from sharing. Recovery has begun to thaw
out our feelings. Sometimes we're not sure if
it is a gift or a curse to be able to feel again. For
most of us, there are times that we become
very aware of our hunger for closeness.

And now we can learn how to fill those
needs, and satisfy that hunger. Friends and
loved ones offer comfort and support when we
feel sad. Now, we can feel safe enough to let
our feelings out and be free.

*Today let me reach out to others and honestly
share my feelings of loneliness.*

The harder the hill is to climb,
the more we enjoy the view from
the top.

Ross Pauly

Each day brings us a new hill to climb and gives us a new view from the top. The ups and downs of living make sense now as we work to get through each day honestly.

Life's rainbows usually don't come all at once, but instead appear in pieces of daily color. As we learn to take a little time to look back on each day, we are able to find some good in our struggle and efforts. Taking life and its challenges in small parts is what recovery is about.

There will be days when we will have the privilege of seeing beauty from the top, but each day is a small hill that we conquer and deserve to enjoy.

Today let me enjoy all of my accomplishments, both big and small.

April 5

All the bridges that you burn
come back one day to haunt you.
One day, you'll find yourself
walking lonely.

Tracy Chapman

In our pain we may have pushed out of our lives the people who loved us most. Full of self-disgust, we may have found it impossible to let others be close to us.

Surveying the wreckage of our past relationships can fill our hearts with pain as we see the hurt in the eyes of the people who used to be there for us. Rebuilding bridges and mending fences is not an overnight project. Trust is like a flower that has to be nurtured and gently watered for it to have the best chance of blooming again. In making amends, we are rebuilding the bridge to ourselves, to our loved ones, and to our new life.

Today let me remember that bridges to friends are easier to patch than replace.

*Those of us who have come to
make regular use of prayer would
no more do without it than we
would refuse air, food, and
sunshine.*

Bill Wilson

Prayer is the fuel that keeps our days
balanced and running smoothly. The more
we pray, the more it seems to become an
automatic part of our day. At first we may
have doubted the power of prayer, but little by
little it is becoming a trusted friend.

Most of the time, our prayers aren't very
fancy or formal. It has been said that even the
worst problems and hardest situations can be
made better through prayer and willingness
on our part to be open to answers. No matter
how big or little our prayer may be, or how
often we say it, we can be assured that it is
always welcomed.

Today let me trust the power of prayer.

April 7

*Angels can fly because they take
themselves lightly.*

G. K. Chesterton

Most of us wonder if we will ever be first
in anything. Many of us don't know what it
feels like to win a prize or be a star in a sport.
We do know what it feels like not to win.

Often, we tend to be too hard on ourselves.
We need to remember that we do have good
qualities even though we may not be first.
This is especially hard for us to believe on the
days when things don't go our way.

Two ideas that help are: Stop comparing,
and keep going. The more we accept ourselves, the more we can accept the new horizons that are opening up for us.

Today let me look for things to enjoy in school.

Don't worry if your job is small,
and your rewards are few:
Remember that the mighty oak,
was once a nut like you.

Anonymous

We feel better about ourselves when we can laugh at ourselves a bit. All it takes is a little attitude adjustment. For example, if I decide to learn to ski and my first day out I fall on my face, I can take the attitude, "I am a klutz, I'm not capable, I don't fit here," or I can take the attitude, "This sport is a riot! What a challenge! I can't wait to feel what it's like to get down without falling."

The person with the first attitude will quit and feel badly about himself or herself. The person with the second attitude may never be an olympic skier, but will have fun, confidence, and a sense of accomplishment.

Today let me remember that attitudes make the difference and attitudes can be changed.

April 9

A good listener is not only popular everywhere, but after awhile he knows something.

Wilson Mizner

Sometimes we talk a lot because no one ever taught us how to listen. Listening is an art anyone can learn. It is also the most important thing we can do for ourselves when we need help. It may be hard to ask for help, but it's also hard to listen to the advice we get when we ask.

We can learn by asking the people who listen to us best how they do it. We can practice by offering a willing ear to another who has asked for our support. And we can reap the rewards of recovery by listening to those we've asked for advice. Soon, we'll develop the ability to listen to our own inner voice, and to our Higher Power. With support like this, we can go a long way.

Today let me be satisfied just to listen.

*I like not only to be loved, but
also to be told that I am loved.*

George Eliot

If we don't ask for what we want, how will
others know? If we want our mothers to stop
nagging us and start praising us for our successes, how will we let them know? If we say
clearly, "Mom, I feel disappointed when you
don't compliment me on what I've done," our
mothers will know how we feel. Stating the
feeling—disappointment—and telling when
it happens is effective communication. It
doesn't guarantee we'll always get what we
want, but it does guarantee that if we don't,
it's not because we didn't communicate well.

We can communicate. We are learning
how good it feels to tell people how we feel and
what we need. Best of all, today we can tell
the people in our lives that we love them.

*Today let me work towards giving clear mes-
sages others can understand.*

April 11

It ain't no use to sit and wonder why, Babe.

Bob Dylan

We can stay stuck in our recovery by asking, "Why?" Keeping it simple means that we are learning to start asking, "How?" instead. When we are willing to ask how we can change something, we get into action and grow. Time stands still and depression sits on our shoulders when we get analysis paralysis and ask only "Why?" The only way to cure analysis paralysis is to take action. We can inventory our lives and see how truly blessed we are.

Today we have a choice. We can spend our time feeling bad about what we didn't get or we can make the most of what we did get.

Today let me spend more time asking how and really living than asking why and merely preparing to live.

Jealousy is a snake that can ruin anyone's day.

Terry McReynolds

Few feelings can tear up a person inside the way jealousy does. When we stay caught in a web of jealousy, it can become an obsession that doesn't want to let go. It has the power to make us sick and ruin our days.

Jealousy punishes us a lot more than it punishes the person we have the feelings about. It gets in the way of any healing that might happen with that person.

The snake of jealousy will stop biting us when we are willing to talk over our feelings with a trustworthy person. It's up to us—do we want pain or peace? Sometimes it takes more strength to let go than to hang on, but our rewards are serenity, humility, and a better feeling about ourselves.

Today let me have the courage and strength to let go.

*I am grateful for every smile,
touch, rainbow, and storm of life.*

Penelope Dewlight

Gratitude is the life saver that will rescue us when our ship is sinking and all else has failed. Some days nothing seems to work for us. The whole day seems designed to do us in. What did we do to deserve this mess? Haven't we been trying hard? Why should this happen to us now? When our path is blocked with fear, we really feel stuck.

When everything seems hopeless, gratitude can help us get unstuck. A few minutes spent thinking about what we have, remembering how bad life once was, can help us realize how much we've gained. A warm home on a cold night, food in an empty stomach, the beauty of the world around us all can help us be grateful.

Today let me be truly grateful.

*Try a thing you haven't tried
before three times; once to get over
the fear, once to find out how to
do it, and a third time to find out
whether you like it or not.*

Virgil Thomas

Overcoming fear calls for acceptance, forgiveness, and action. First, we truly accept and forgive ourselves for being afraid. If we believe that facing our fear is in our best interest, then we act. We will still feel fear, but we feel the fear and do it anyway.

If we wait until we understand perfectly and are completely free of our fears, we might never take action. As we face our biggest fears, they lose their power to harm us and they teach us the strength of our deep personal resources.

Today let me face at least one fear.

The key to everything is patience.
You get the chicken by hatching
the egg—not by smashing it.

Arnold Glasow

We are impatient people. We want what we want, now!

Now we're beginning to learn that patience pays big rewards. Waiting one more day may help us avoid a relapse. Waiting for people we care for can help us avoid destructive friendships. Saving for something we want gives us an added bonus: we feel better about ourselves and have more self-respect. And as we learn to love ourselves more, we find we don't need things to be happy, we just need our own self-respect.

Now we know how to be patient. We patiently work through our recovery and know how much a little patience can pay us back.

Today let me care enough about myself to be patient.

*Let us praise You in the way You
love best, by shining on those
around us. Let us preach You not
by words, but by our example.*

Mother Teresa's Prayer

Living our life well is the best gift we can
ever give to others. "Walking the walk" works
better than "talking the talk." When we give
up drugs and alcohol, we offer hope to others.
A wise man once said that he goes to meetings
to find the one thing he relates to instead of
looking for all the ways he is different.

Every day we are given the opportunity to
offer service to others around us and to be a
good example. When we live sobriety we help
not only ourselves but also our families, our
friends, and those we meet at meetings.

*Today let me promote my recovery program by
sharing with others the ways in which my life
is getting better.*

Worry: Putting today's sun under tomorrow's cloud.

Anonymous

We used to believe that worry would magically protect us. If we worried enough about something, maybe it wouldn't happen. This old way failed us. Now we know all worry can do for us is wear us down. Now we know that actions, not thoughts, make things happen. If we do the next right thing, we'll find the strength and support to handle life, whatever comes our way. We've found a Higher Power to help us. Letting go of worry is a big relief.

Today let me stop worrying and learn to trust my Higher Power.

What kind of love do you want to attract? . . . Develop those quali-ties in yourself and you will attract a person who has them.

Louise Hay

Love is like a butterfly that lights on our shoulder when we least expect it. The more we are able to relax in our day-to-day lives and really be ourselves, the more attractive we are to others.

Trying to find the perfect person to love by analyzing everyone we meet to see who passes the test makes it hard for people to touch our hearts. Instead of taking an inventory of others, we can now become the kind of person we find lovable. And that gives us enough freedom to stop playing games. As we relax, we find that we are open to the deeper and more lovely qualities in others.

Today let me focus on the love I have to give life instead of the love I want from life.

April 19

There are only two lasting bequests we can hope to give our children. One of these is roots; the other, wings.

Hodding Carter

We probably had some needs that were not met. Maybe we needed more physical attention—maybe we got too much of the wrong kind of physical attention. Maybe nobody encouraged us. That little boy or girl who needed something is still in us. Even though we're grown up, that past is still a part of us and we need to nurture that child within.

We can give ourselves what we missed as children. We can offer ourselves praise when we do well, and gentleness when we make a mistake. We can treat ourselves with the same respect and affection we'd give to another. We can make a new, loving world for the child who still lives within us.

Today let me nurture the child within me.

To every disadvantage there is a corresponding advantage.

W. Clement Stone

At first, we might see recovery as giving up the things we care about. But in a few weeks or months, we start to find all the things we've gained. Being able to sleep soundly at night. Providing what we need for ourselves, instead of being dependent on other people. Feeling strong instead of feeling weak. Feeling in control of our lives instead of feeling controlled by life. We begin to feel the true value of friendship and sharing with people who care about us. We begin to look forward to a brighter tomorrow.

A whole new world is waiting for us. Peace and serenity fill our days and our dreams. And we find that for each thing we gave up, we've gained more in return.

Today help me concentrate on the gains of recovery.

Life is what happens while you
are making other plans.

John Lennon

Spiritual awakenings are not always giant, thunderous revelations of sickness and healing, but rather little bursts of joy throughout our lives. These little bursts of joy are spiritual because they touch at the core of our being.

The more we work on our sobriety, the more of those bursts of joy we'll experience. Part of it is because we're starting to experience feelings again and part of it is a gift, the treasures that true sobriety brings. We are beginning to see the small ways God works in our lives each day. Now we can take time to look for and experience the bursts of joy that are offered to us as we begin to know our true selves.

Today let me look for reasons to rejoice.

*. . . she'll bring out the best and
the worst you can be.*

Billy Joel

Falling in love gives us an opportunity to grow. When we open up and get close to someone, we are vulnerable. We are close to our feelings. Love does expose the best and the worst in us. We need to nourish and enjoy our best sides, but what do we do about the worst in us?

Some of us are afraid that if we really get close to someone, they might leave us. Fear of being abandoned can set our emotions off like a firecracker. We are learning to live one day at a time, and we can apply this to relationships as well. This means being honest each day, and carefully opening ourselves up to another, a bit at a time. Now we can take the time to let a relationship grow and blossom.

Today let me rejoice in relationships.

April 23

The longer I live, the more beauti-
ful life becomes.

Frank Lloyd Wright

No deal to make, no excuses to make, no
lies to tell, nothing to cover up, no trouble to
get out of, nothing to steal, no need to manipulate, no wondering what happened the night
before, no explosions, scenes, or frightening
horrors. This is the picture of serenity.

Serenity doesn't mean there won't be
rough times, it just means there won't be
preventable, unending, ongoing rough times.
Serenity means waking up in the morning
without fear and agitation.

Our fearful days are over. Now we can
face life with peace and strength. Today, we
know we can take care of ourselves and our
lives, whatever comes our way.

Today let me appreciate serenity.

The only place where success comes before work is in a dictionary.

Vidal Sassoon

Most of us get our riches the old fashioned way—we must earn them. Whether it's sobriety, a new car, or a new outfit. It's true we all get lucky breaks now and then, but the most treasured prizes are the ones we've earned. They mean so much more. Getting a gift is a joyous surprise, but the feeling is different than when we work to achieve something.

We worked hard for our sobriety and for our happiness. No one gave it to us, and no one can take it away. What a feeling of joy and accomplishment that brings us today.

Today let me be willing to work for what I want.

April 25

*The only thing we have to fear is
fear itself.*

Franklin D. Roosevelt

Fear is contagious and can actually be
passed down through generations. How do
our parents approach life? With fear and
dread or with hope and anticipation? If our
parents were fearful we might be the same.
Perhaps our parents' fear was instilled in
them by their parents.

Nothing limits our recovery as much as
fear and negativity. When we look on the
dark side, it's easy to miss the daily miracles.
Fear is powerful, but it can be overcome.

We can always depend on our Higher
Power to help us through our fearful times
and lead us to life's joys.

*Today let me believe that my Higher Power
will help me through fear to joy.*

*My doctor gave me two weeks to
live. I hope they're in August.*

Ronnie Shakes

Growing up with a dysfunctional family
hurts and is scary. We want to get help but we
don't know how.

In time, we can learn to nurture ourselves, to give ourselves what we missed as
children. We'll never get childhood back again,
but we can become healthy adults and put
childhood behind us. In time, we may even
find a way to forgive those who hurt us.

Remembering and talking about the pain
is the only way to begin to heal. We only need
to find the courage to take our secrets out of
the closet. We are not alone. We are entering
the best years of our lives, and we are becoming, day by day, more able to enjoy them.

*Today let me remember that there is no pain
too big to heal.*

April 27

Own your own pain. . .
Give it a name.
What you possess
Cannot possess you.

Patricia Ruth Schwartz

Pain is the soil in which the seeds of our recovery lie scattered. We sometimes do get sick of hearing "no pain, no gain."

Identifying the sources of our pain is the beginning of healing. When we have a toothache, we first need to locate the hurting tooth. Emotional aches are often harder to identify and discover. We sometimes want to protect ourselves from knowing the whole truth.

We are learning to be fearless and honest in our recovery. Soul searching is the necessary detective work of recovery. Pain that we face can be beaten.

Today let me remember that what hurts me most are buried secrets.

*Miracles sometimes occur, but one
has to work terribly hard for
them.*

Chaim Weizmann

The funny thing about miracles is that we usually have to earn them. We've all heard someone say something like this, "It's a miracle that I passed history, I didn't study for the final." That may sound like a miracle, but the person probably did attend class, take notes, and study for all the other tests. The same is true of sobriety. It seems like a miracle, but sobriety is something we earn every day we don't drink or use and each time we go to meetings.

The opportunities in life are the miracles. We are presented with them every day, and it's up to each of us to make it happen.

Today let me see the opportunity for miracles in my life.

April 29

*Life consists not in holding good
cards, but in playing those you do
hold well.*

Josh Billings

Many of us are shy. It's hard to believe
because we don't seem shy. That's because we
hide our shyness from those around us. We
may have acted cool and used drugs to help us
feel less shy. But there hasn't been a product
made yet that cures shyness.

If we're shy and it doesn't interfere with
our lives, then it might be best to accept that
part of ourselves. If our shyness bothers us,
then we can get help with it. Friends, counselors, other recovering people, books, and
our families can help if we ask.

We're in charge of our lives now, and we
can decide our futures. We can learn to accept
and love ourselves. Or we can use our new
experiences, knowledge, and friends to change.

Today let me play my cards well.

*It isn't the trauma that makes us
sick. It's the inability to talk
about the trauma.*

Alice Miller

Sharing our problems is one way to get rid
of our internal garbage. It has been said that
we are as sick as the secret we keep. If we
can't talk about our secrets with someone, we
can at least write them out. Since no one else
will ever need to see what we have written, we
can be completely honest about what we think
and how we feel. If we have turned our wills
and lives over to the care of God, we have
nothing to be afraid of.

By honestly sharing what we think and
feel, we are admitting that we own these
thoughts and feelings, and they are part of
our lives. Anything that we own we can give
away. What we get in return is freedom.

*Today let me have the courage to share a secret
fear.*

*Friendship is always a sweet
responsibility, never an
opportunity.*

Kahlil Gibran

We have friends who are very special to
us. They care about us but in different ways.
Some may want the best for us and are quick
to give us advice. Others may want the best
for us and help us believe that we would know
what was best for us. We will always end up
on the doorstep of the second friends when
times get rough.

It is so wonderful to know that someone
loves us enough to take the time to really hear
us and hand us back our own strengths and
resources. When we are vulnerable we need
to lean on friends but not be carried. We can
learn to be good friends in this way too, and to
be responsible only for our own lives. This is
part of the new freedom of our recovery.

Today let me be a true friend to others.

*The only way to have a friend is
to be a friend.*

> *Ralph Waldo Emerson*

Love is sharing. We feel great about our recovery, and we want to announce it to someone we love. Sharing our joy can happen in romantic love or friendship love. It's sharing with someone who will share back, someone who accepts us, someone who wants to see us happy, and someone who we're totally comfortable with and not trying to impress. This is what love is. We don't have to wait for romantic love. We can feel that sharing with a friend we love, too.

We are free now to be happy enough with ourselves to love and share with others. We can see the beauty in others and rejoice in it.

Today let me cherish the loving relationships in my life.

May 3

*There are fifty things I want to
say to my parents: "Let me grow
up!" (Repeat 49 times.)*

A frustrated teenager

Nothing makes us more angry than feeling like our parents don't trust us. Sometimes we feel like they were never young themselves. Sometimes we get so tired of their rules. We feel a need to make our own paths and to be loved and accepted for exactly who we are. We are growing, learning, changing people who make mistakes and learn through trial and error. They want to help us to do right, but we need to learn how our own way.

We can help our parents see us for who we really are by seeing them as they really are. We are able today to state our needs while truly listening to them. Now we can start to build a healthy relationship with our parents.

Today let me share one honest part of me with my parents.

No one can make you feel inferior without your consent.

Eleanor Roosevelt

In this moment, we are the best we can be. Today, we can work at loving the best in ourselves and not fearing the worst. We are truly wonderful and growing people with gifts and qualities that make us who we are. No one can make us feel inferior without our consent.

Now, we are in charge of our lives and growth. We can choose to let go of old negative thinking. We can choose to think positive, loving thoughts about ourselves. We never need to be victims again—to addiction or to other people. We have options today. We can choose to grow in a positive recovery program. We can choose to have loving, affirming people in our lives.

Today I will stick with the winners. I am a winner today and every day.

*I am glad I did it, partly because
it was well worth it, and chiefly
because I shall never have to do it
again.*

Mark Twain

When we first think about making amends, we think our egos will explode. We take a big drink of humility when we make amends for our actions. The hardest part of making amends is just making the decision to face the music and do it.

Being newly clean and sober, we sometimes have a hard time being objective about some situations. Sponsors and friends can be of great help to us here.

Making amends is a positive way to free ourselves from the past. We can be proud of ourselves for taking a giant step in keeping our lives on an optimistic road to tomorrow.

Today let me become willing to make amends to one person.

*There is guidance for each of us,
and by only listening, we shall
hear the right word.*

Ralph Waldo Emerson

We can be grateful today that we are able to sit still long enough to hear who we really are. We can get to know ourselves for the first time. We still have times that are rushed and hurried, but we also have quiet times to think and meditate. We have balance.

Deep inside us we have all the answers. We know what we need to feel good about ourselves. Now, we have the time and the tools to make friends with ourselves. Now, we can learn to love ourselves as we are. Now, we are listening.

Today let me take some time to listen.

May 7

*T'aint worthwhile to wear a day
all out before it comes.*

Sarah Orne Jewett

We might be tempted to moan and groan about how horrible it's going to be. But this means we ruin today by worrying about tomorrow and we could end up ruining every day.

Many of us like to do things big. We think and worry about everything rather than just doing one thing right for one day. We lost many todays worrying about tomorrow. Now we know how foolish that can be. There is always something good that we can do for ourselves today. The moment we are living is the only one we have. Now, we can live for today, instead of yesterday and tomorrow. We can let go of our mistakes. We can plan for our future.

Today let me respect this day.

It is okay to feel relieved and even happy when someone dies. It is okay to feel whatever is real.

Robert Kavanaugh

How could anyone feel happy when someone dies? It's possible. Maybe we are happy to see someone die who has been suffering. It is good to see them have peace from pain. We are not wishing them dead. We are wishing an end to their pain.

We may feel happy, sad, resentful, joyful, all in a single day. None of those feelings are good or bad. We can choose to act on our feelings, and choose how we will act, or we can choose not to act at all. Our feelings don't decide what we will do any more.

Now we can see our feelings realistically. We can accept our feelings in whatever way they come and learn to go on.

Today let me look at my feelings of guilt and fear calmly and realistically.

Never, "for the sake of peace and quiet," deny your own experience or conviction.

        Dag Hammarskjold

People-pleasing at the expense of our own needs can make us sick. Letting our personal wells run dry causes a spiritual thirst that no amount of people-pleasing can satisfy.

Sometimes we stop saying what's on our minds because we're afraid to make someone else mad. We do anything for peace and quiet, especially if we think that what we need or feel might not please someone else. We let others become our gods, and inside we feel like scared little kids.

Honestly telling people how we feel helps both them and us. They know where we stand and we acknowledge our feelings. Others may not always agree with us, but they will learn to respect us.

Today let me say what's on my mind.

It's the most unhappy people who most fear change.

              Mignon McLaughlin

Sometimes we keep making the same mistakes over and over again. This is denial in action. There is something about ourselves, our program, our past, our inner lives that is being denied. If we're really honest about trying to grow, we won't stay in denial very long. If we decide we'd rather do it our way and not learn and grow and change from it, we're denying and will keep our defects of character working against us, leading us to the same old place they've always led us.

But we don't have to do that. We can grow and change our old patterns. Each day gives us a new opportunity to discover ourselves and discover ways we can change for the better.

Today let me make one change in my life.

Love seeketh only Self to please.

William Blake

Planning and making decisions about the future takes courage. It may be a real struggle trying to decide what goal we want to pursue. Sometimes we made false starts because we thought of others first. What did our parents want us to be? What careers pay the most? The most important question of all is,"What do I really want for me?"

What are our gifts and talents? What makes us happy? Today we can plan our plans and dream our dreams. We can honestly look at ourselves, see our strengths and our weaknesses. Then we can make a choice based on what and who we are.

Today let me plan my own plans and dream my own dreams for the future.

*The protection of our rights can
endure no longer than the per-
formance of our responsibilities.*

John F. Kennedy

Sometimes it feels like everyone is telling
us what to do—parents, teachers, bosses. Most
of us don't like being told what to do. We're old
enough to know what we're doing, we say.

It helps to remember that many of us
haven't earned the right to make decisions on
our own yet. We got into so much trouble that
our parents, teachers, and employers lost
faith in us.

We prove ourselves by being responsible.
We'll be given more freedom, but we have to
earn it first. When someone tells us what to
do, we can pray for the patience to accept it
with a positive frame of mind and the knowledge that we're growing up.

*Today let me accept powerlessness in at least
one small way.*

May 13

*He started to sing as he tackled
the thing that couldn't be done,
and he did it.*

Edgar A. Guest

There once was a commercial on TV with a timeless message. A woman in the commercial can't make up her mind between jogging, aerobics, weight training, and basketball. While she's going back and forth trying to decide, a little voice keeps saying, "Just do it!"

This message speaks to all of us in recovery. So often we talk everything to death, but we forget to plain just do it! If we would just change and show the change by our actions, our problems would be solved. What a joy it is for us now to be able to change.

Today I'll try to think of something that it's time to do, and stop talking, thinking, or deciding about it.

*They started to fight when the
money got tight.*

Billy Joel

We are told we should inventory money,
relationships, and self-esteem when having
problems with our sobriety. Not getting honest
about money can keep us on the edge of
recovery. Worry about money and paying
bills can actually get us high. When any area
of our life is out of balance, we're in trouble.

Getting honest about money can start
with a written inventory. What does money
really mean to us today? What did it mean in
the past? Do we want to change? How can we
do that? Our attitude about money can help
us or hurt us, but now we have a choice. We
can choose how we'll feel about money, and
what we can do to change. Today, the choice
is ours.

*Today let me be free from fear and worry about
money.*

May 15

*There is nothing worse than
waking up in the morning and
remembering that you've had a
fight with your best friend.*

Joan Williams

Friends can be really confusing. It seems like one day they love us and the next they don't. When a good friend is angry, it feels like a kick in the stomach. At first it feels too hard to really talk about it with the friend, so instead of confronting the problem, we just hope it will go away. Problems usually don't just go away, though.

Our friends are so important they are worth taking the risk of having an honest talk with. When we finally get the courage to confront the situation with an open mind and listening heart, true friendships have a deep ability to heal.

Today let me be open and honest with my friends.

*Take sides. Neutrality helps the
oppressor, never the victim.
Silence encourages the tormentor,
never the tormented.*

Elie Wiesel

Learning what we want to stand up for
and what we want to speak out against is
hard, but it is worth the work it takes. Our
hearts sing when we speak up for our values.

Coming to hear and accept the voice of our
intuition and sense of values allows us to give
our feelings the power of assertive words and
positive actions. What a great discovery to
learn that we can get our views across without attacking others.

Sitting on the fence of life gives us blis-
ters. When we make a commitment to be true
to ourselves, we have only one person to
please—ourselves.

*Today let me have the courage to take a stand
and speak out for what I believe.*

There is so much good in the worst of us, and there is so much bad in the best of us, that it hardly becomes any of us to talk about the rest of us.

Edward Wallis Hoch

It has often been said that when we meet someone we can't stand, it's because there is something about that person that reminds us of ourselves. When we judge others, we take a risk. Judgment seems to blow up our own egos and gives us a false sense of our own worth. Do I really want to feel good about myself by putting someone else down?

Today we can decide to focus on finding one positive quality in the person who irritates us the most. When we focus on finding the good, we have less energy for negative thinking. When we focus on the good, we are exercising the better part of our vision.

Today let me look for the best in all people.

The essence of heroism is self-trust.

Ralph Waldo Emerson

Getting sober and healthy in our spirits and minds is hard work. Since the hardest battles to win are those inside ourselves, we must also take responsibility for rewarding ourselves too. A good reward might be thinking of everything we may gain if we stick to our program and don't give up. We can think ahead and try to realize how good we'll feel about ourselves. We can let ourselves feel proud and strong. These rewards come from inside us. Our friends will surely be happy for us, and that will feel good. But we'll be the one who gets the biggest reward

Today let me be happy for myself and my recovery.

Think about it. There must be a
Higher Love, down in the heart or
hidden in the stars above.

Steve Winwood

Love is always with us. It is like a thread that attaches us to a limitless goodness and grace. Sometimes we need to become love detectives to stay in touch with the current of love in our lives.

Love detectives look for the clues of love in everyday situations. When we enter a room we can practice looking for the beauty instead of the ugliness. When we meet a new person, we can learn to focus on the attractive things instead of all the things that may be wrong. The secret of being a love detective is to practice bringing our most positive eyes into every situation. As we radiate love, it flows back to us. Love will always be with us as we open ourselves up to its everyday song.

Today let me believe in the presence of love.

*Happiness is not a state to arrive
at, but a manner of traveling.*

Margaret Lee Runbeck

We know happiness has to come from
inside. Still, sometimes we get conned into
believing we'll be really happy if we can get a
car, or go out with someone we have our eye
on, or buy a certain piece of clothing.

Today we can make a real, honest effort to
find happiness in our hearts, deep down where
our values live and our love comes from.
Today we can see how far we've come, how
many good changes we've made, how much
we've learned in recovery. This is a happy
event money can't buy.

*Today let me remember the only one respon-
sible for my happiness is me.*

Life has a way of setting things in order and leaving them be. Very tidy, is life.

Jean Anouilh

When we attack and try to force things to happen, we usually end up frustrated. We can cooperate with the laws of nature and flow of time, or we can push other people, places, and things to get what we want.

We are finding that we are poor competition for the natural flow life seems to create. The more we learn of living, the more we experience a purposeful rhythm to existence. The truth of the matter is that we are painfully coming to realize we are not in charge.

Now, we're learning we are responsible only for ourselves, and just one day at a time. What new freedom we find in this simple idea! Now we can let go, and let God.

Today let me gently do the footwork of living.

In these times you have to be an optimist to open your eyes in the morning.

Carl Sandburg

For some of us morning is the worst time of day. Anyone who has ever had the morning blues will understand the feeling. But a hard morning doesn't have to mean a hard day.

We can change the day by changing our attitude. Instead of dwelling on dark, negative thoughts, we can look forward to the good things a new day might bring. A few minutes of meditation or a pleasant thought about a loved friend can help brighten things up.

We can change gloom, a little, if we look for something good. As we make progress in recovery, more good will come our way.

Today let me remember that my days will get better as I get better.

*Too many people are ready to
carry the stool when there is a
piano to be moved.*

Anonymous

"I have to stop mixing my drinks." "It must've been some bad stuff." These phrases probably sound familiar. We sound like this when we want to carry the stool, but are not willing to move the piano. When we talked like this, we were denying the problem and avoiding help.

If we are to experience all the joys of recovery, we must be alert to the piano that needs moving. In other words, if we want all of the benefits of getting help, we must get all the help, not just the little pieces here and there we decide to pick up. Today, we need to be willing to do the hard work of recovery as well as the easy and enjoyable work. Now we can. Now we are ready.

Today let me move the piano.

*Knowledge of what is possible is
the beginning of happiness.*

George Santayana

Happy, joyous, and free. We hear about
these in recovery. We wonder how there can
be happiness after all we've been through.

Happiness is possible in recovery because
we come to understand what is possible for us
through recovery. We can be happy because
we're still alive. Some of our friends aren't.
We can be happy that we are regaining our
health, and we can be happy because we are
making new friends who really care for us.

Most of all, we can be happy because we
are free. In recovery, we find an entirely new
kind of freedom. It is not a distorted freedom
that disregards everyone and everything
except ourselves. It is the wonderful freedom
to love ourselves and to love others. All of this
is possible. And we are happy.

Today let me see the possibilities in my life.

May 25

*There is no one who subsists by
himself alone.*

Owen Felltham

No one can recover for us. We depend on
others for support and guidance, but we alone
are responsible for our well-being. It's our job
to use the new tools of recovery. It's our job to
know when to ask for help.

Sometimes it gets confusing because on
the one hand, we're told that we're supposed
to depend on sponsors. How are we supposed
to be independent and dependent at the same
time? We depend on others to give us guidance so we can take independent actions.

The tools are there, but we must use
them. It takes courage and independence to
admit we need help and then ask for it. We
have that courage today and with it we are
gaining our independence.

*Today I will work toward independence by
accepting guidance.*

*In our hearts we are all the same.
We get into trouble when we think
we are less or better than each
other.*

Happy Harper

When we were using, our moods often
went from feeling very bad and wrong about
ourselves, to feeling better than other people.
It was hard for us to keep a balance between
those two extremes.

This is a very hard seesaw to be on. We
really didn't know how to feel about ourselves
and other people.

Today we know we're just people. We
won't be right all the time, but we won't be
wrong all the time either. Today we can be
ourselves—no better and no worse than anyone else. What a relief that is.

*Today let me be grateful for the sameness of
spirit I share with all the people in my world.*

May 27

*A sound mind in a sound body is
a short but full description of a
happy state in this world.*

John Locke

It's important to keep our bodies and spirits well and healthy. If we don't get enough sleep, we may become moody and sluggish. If we fill our bodies with junk food, our bodies' hunger systems will be upset and start telling us we're hungry when we're not.

Many of us fail at attempts to keep ourselves in balance because we have an all-or-nothing attitude. We go on severe diets, we exercise until we drop, and in general try to be perfect. The object, though, should be balance—not perfection.

We don't have to live like that today. We can balance our lives and be kind to both our bodies and our spirits. Today we can be well.

Today let me do something that is good for my body and my spirit.

*God is not a cosmic bellboy for
whom we can press a button to
get things done.*

Harry Emerson Fosdick

Trusting our Higher Power doesn't mean
that we sit back and do nothing. It means we
also do our part. We know that one way God
guides us is through other people. Doing our
part means doing all the basics. We work on
our recovery. We talk to people who can help
us. When we do all these things, we find that
God does speak to us. Friends give us sugges-
tions we would not have thought of ourselves.

Sometimes the answers to our problems
aren't so obvious. We are confused about how
to deal with some things. After we've done all
we can do, we can stop searching for the
solutions and trust our Higher Power to make
things fall into place. And He does.

Today I will do my part so God can help me.

An optimist is one who makes the best of it when he gets the worst of it.

Laurence J. Peter

Optimism is a contagious gift we can pass on to others. We can choose how we view our worlds. We have the choice each morning about the way we are going to face our days. We can choose to feel negative and depressed, or we can choose to expect the best for the next 24 hours.

There is a great power in positive thinking. If we are unsure of how to handle any situation we are going to face, we can rehearse what we would like to have happen. We can practice seeing positive results. We can see ourselves confident and happy and full of energy. What we see is what we get.

Today let me be optimistic.

*Affliction comes to us, not to
make us sad but sober; not to
make us sorry but wise.*

Henry Ward Beecher

We often meet people who seem to have escaped all the garbage we've been through—people whose most painful childhood memory was of throwing up in the third grade. When this happens, it is helpful to remember that we are all shaped by some suffering. It is only through overcoming obstacles that we grow. People who have suffered and endured and then overcome an obstacle are strong souls because they've been tested. They don't teach wisdom at school or in books. Wisdom comes from living, struggling, and enduring.

We are wise now and will grow more so in our recovery. Our spirits are not shallow and unexplored. Our spirits are deep and scarred but wiser and stronger for the suffering.

Today let me grow strong and wise.

*He who has health has hope, and
he who has hope has everything.*

Arabian Proverb

Part of our program today is taking good
care of ourselves physically. When we were
using, we abused our bodies in a lot of ways.
We didn't eat right, didn't sleep regularly,
and rarely exercised.

But today is different. We can eat regular
meals, things that are good for us. We can
exercise, whether it's taking a walk with
friends, or playing basketball, or doing situps.
We can sleep regular hours. We feel better
when we take care of ourselves.

Taking good care of our physical selves is
a way to care for our emotional selves as well.
It is a way we take control once again of our
lives by doing what we can to practice self-
love.

*Today let me take time to eat well and get some
exercise.*

*Shame keeps grown up people
feeling like helpless five-year-olds.*

Sam Friend

Shame is a feeling that can paralyze us. When we feel ashamed, we feel worthless. We often feel ashamed about our past. We sometimes feel we are bad. We may feel like mistakes. Shame can be a clog in our emotional lives that stops the flow of other feelings. Sometimes when we start to talk about our shame, we seem to get numb.

But shame can only live in silence. Talking with a trusted friend can help change our feelings of shame into acceptance. We may find others have felt the same way and they can share how they changed their feelings of shame to self-acceptance. Our feelings of shame can fade. We can't change the past, but we can change the future.

Today let me trust that there is a difference in my life.

*Much human suffering is related
to the false expectation that we
are called to take each other's
loneliness away.*

Henri Nouwen

Many of us have a hunger of the spirit that can't seem to get filled by people or chemicals. There is a part of each of us that will always be alone and longing for something or someone who seems just out of reach.

We can find peace and serenity inside ourselves, though. We're longing for love because we need to love ourselves. We feel lonely because we haven't learned to enjoy our own company. But we can learn to love ourselves and end our own loneliness. We can learn to forgive ourselves for our past, and plan good things for our future. Then we can learn to make our own dreams come true.

Today let me ask my Higher Power to fill me with peace.

There is a mountain,
There is a sea,
There is you and there is me.

Warren J. Harrity

Sometimes falling in love seems to make time stop. Lovers get so centered on each other that the rest of the world seems to vanish. We want to isolate with the beloved and soak up every minute of precious time.

Problems can begin when we lose the balance between love and the rest of the world. When we become obsessed with love and give up our friends and interests, we're in trouble.

When we feel that way, we need to work to avoid isolation and obsession. There's a great big world out there just waiting for us to rejoin it. We can find balance there. We learn we can fall in love and still keep our hold on balance.

Today let me try to be balanced in my relationships.

*I am, indeed, a king, because I
know how to rule myself.*

Pietro Aretino

Long before a relapse, our thinking changes. We neglect our program in small ways and our attitude becomes negative.

We may be losing perspective and thinking about the old days as good days. When that happens, we can try to remember what things were really like. We can relive the pain and fear and lack of control. And we can realize how different life is for us now.

How good we feel knowing we are in charge of our lives! Today we can feel pride and self-love. Today, we can change our thinking and catch ourselves before we are out of control. We don't have to live that way any more. We have changed, and we will keep making progress every day.

Today let me value and protect my recovery.

There is only one corner of the universe you can be certain of improving, and that's yourself.

Aldous Huxley

One way to increase our self-esteem is practice. Doing such things as trying something new, doing something we used to be fearful of, making a difficult phone call, or trying a new haircut or style of clothing is a start.

If we do something each day to stretch ourselves, to take a little risk, eventually our self-esteem grows. The miracle is we stop caring about the outcome and start caring more about the doing and how good it feels to grow. Before long, we feel the change in ourselves as our power over our own lives grows.

Today let me stretch myself a little.

June 6

*All the knowledge I possess
everyone else can acquire, but my
heart is all my own.*

Johann von Goethe

Now that we're in recovery, learning about ourselves is a new experience. Finding out how we really feel and being true to those feelings is critical to our self-esteem and our sobriety. What do we like and dislike? How do we really feel about things? To answer these questions we need to stay alert to our feelings as they hit us.

Sometimes finding out about ourselves takes time and experimenting. We try new things and look deep inside ourselves to learn how we feel. This process of discovering who we are is an adventure. We won't like everything we find, but we can learn to love ourselves even with our faults.

Today let me discover how I really feel, and who I really am.

*Fear, the worst of all enemies, can
be effectively cured by forced
repetition of acts of courage.*

Napoleon Hill

We can practice courage over and over
again until we feel some of our fear leaving.
We can learn a lot about courage by watching
newcomers in the program. Every time they
speak and share a little piece of their troubles,
they take a giant step away from fear. When
we see a newcomer hang around after a
meeting and risk talking, we know we are
seeing a courageous act. When we see someone risk, we also see someone grow.

Growing and changing are the rewards
that courage gives back. We get the biggest
rewards when we risk and let another person
really know us. We never see much of fear
when two people are honestly together.

*Today let me remember that courage beats
fear at its own game.*

*Thank you for the stars, moon,
and sun. Thank you for flowers,
birds, and soft winds. Thank you
for my life.*

Penelope Murphy

Many of us came from homes that weren't exactly nice. Many of us created lives for ourselves that were even less nice. We became very good at seeing what we didn't like in life. We were glad to point out the negatives to whomever would listen. Nothing good ever happened. But did it?

For most of us plenty of good happened. We stayed basically healthy against all odds. We are smart and we can learn. What we really need to learn is to look for the good things and appreciate what we have. We need to be able to see the foundation before we can build on it.

Today let me be grateful for one of my assets.

When I give, I give myself.

Walt Whitman

Since we began to recover, many of us have gotten a lot of satisfaction out of helping others. It makes us feel good because it's so different from our old behavior. When we were drinking and drugging, we used people. We manipulated them to get what we wanted. We were always out for ourselves.

Today we're different. We get a lot of pleasure out of being nice. We feel good when others comment on how much we've changed. Many of us find pleasure in being helpful to others. We've learned we can't change anyone but ourselves, and we know how to let go. But we've also found the reward of being a positive force in helping others who want to change. And in giving, we find we've been given a rare and wonderful gift.

Today let me help others when I can.

June 10

*And when they had taken up the
anchors, they committed themselves unto the sea. . .and hoisted
up the mainsail to the wind.*

Acts 27:40

We know today that our Higher Power is
there for us every moment. He loves us
exactly as we are in this second. He carries us
into the winds of life.

We are learning to trust that we are
worthy of His care. We don't have to be anything special to be loved by God. God walks
beside us through the messes and joys of our
lives.

Today we are willing to make fewer
messes. We want to let go of every old habit
that keeps us from being all we can be. We
commit fully to life today knowing that we
will be protected and guarded every step of
the way.

Today let me let go with God and feel safe.

Sometimes even to live is an act of courage.

Seneca

Our idea of courage has changed since we've been in recovery. We used to think we were courageous doing the wild things we did when we were using. Now we realize getting sober and living sober are courageous.

Asking for help was hard. And then being willing to go against the crowd, to stay away from our old friends, to be ridiculed by some of them—that was very hard. Taking an honest look at how we used to be, telling someone all our secrets also took real courage.

By ourselves, we couldn't have done all these things. But today we have a Higher Power who gives us courage to do the things we can't do on our own. With this help, we can do it.

Today let me be courageous.

June 12

*What then is your duty? What
the day demands.*

Johann von Goethe

One of the hardest things for us is taking
responsibility for doing the things we should
do, not just the things we want to do. Before,
we only did what we wanted to do. If we
wanted to get high, we got high. If we didn't
want to go to work or school, we didn't. Often,
we lied or asked others to cover for us.

We can't live that way any more. Sometimes it's hard. We slip back into wanting to
do only the easy things, the fun things. Now
we know life isn't like that. The more we fight
against the things we don't want to do, the
worse they seem. If we just go ahead and do
them, they're over in no time. Then we still
have the energy we used to waste avoiding
things. We can go on to the fun things and
enjoy them. This is what growing up is about.

Today let me do first things first.

*Nothing on earth consumes a
man more quickly than the
passion of resentment.*

Friedrich Nietzsche

Sometimes we get mad and hold onto
resentments. But we know we have to change
that to stay sober. We may want to drink
when we're mad. So letting go of anger is
really a life-and-death issue.

What is important today is being able to
talk about the things that bother us. We used
to sit and brood about things for days, getting
more and more furious. Now, we can call a
friend and talk the problem out. It feels good
just to talk it out. Then we try to let it go. We
know that if we don't, we put our serenity and
sobriety in jeopardy. No matter what we're
mad about, it's not worth that.

Today let me let go of a resentment.

June 14

*Use what language you will, you
can never say anything but what
you are.*

Ralph Waldo Emerson

One of the most important things we're
learning in the program is to express our
feelings. We never realized how hard that
was going to be. We used to think we were
pretty open, but that was often a lot of hot air.
Sure, we could tell someone off if we were
mad, but we couldn't sit down, look someone
calmly in the face, and say how we felt about
something that happened.

But now we're different. We can talk
about our feelings. We can tell someone when
our feelings are hurt, or when we feel rejected.
We could never do that before. We can even
walk up to a friend, give him or her a hug, and
say "I love you." That's the best part of all.

Today let me express my feelings to a friend.

He that conceals his grief finds no remedy for it.

Turkish Proverb

Some days we feel sad. Somehow we got the idea we weren't supposed to feel sad. It's okay to feel happy about things, or even mad, but being sad is hard to deal with.

Sometimes we're sad because we're lonely. Other times we're sad because something sad happens. Whatever the reason for sadness, we can be thankful to be in recovery in those moments. We can get on the phone and talk to a friend. That usually makes us feel better. We can put on paper what is going on inside us. We can pray and turn it over to our Higher Power. After that, the feeling of sadness is usually gone. We don't have to fight it, just work our program with it, like we do with all our problems. And soon we feel better.

Today let me work my sadness through with help.

June 16

Be a friend to thyself, and others
will be so too.

Thomas Fuller

Thinking positive things about ourselves doesn't come naturally. We think we're too dumb, too clumsy, not handsome or pretty enough. Even before we used, we may have felt that we weren't as good as other people.

In recovery, we are gradually changing this. We have new friends who seem to like us just as we are. They see our good qualities. Other people are also responding differently to us now that we're sober. Teachers may give us more compliments at school. We may be getting compliments at work.

Now that other people aren't putting us down, let's stop putting ourselves down. Then we allow ourselves to hear, from ourselves and from others, the good things about us.

Today let me respect myself and see my good qualities.

*If we let things terrify us, life will
not be worth living.*

Seneca

A panic attack is feeling a sudden burst of
anxiety and fear for no reason. We all experience anxiety from time to time but it can
usually be traced to a cause. A true panic
attack happens out of the blue.

Once we may have reacted to panic attacks by getting high and running from them.
Then we'd come down and the whole cycle
would start over.

Now we don't have to react this way. We
can recognize panic attacks for what they are,
isolated happenings that will pass. We can
also get help from friends, counselors, and
sponsors. Today, we are not alone in our fear.
We have hope.

Today let me remember not to panic.

June 18

Kindness in words creates confidence. Kindness in thinking creates profoundness. Kindness in giving creates love.

Lao-tzu

Some people seem to be naturally kind and gentle and aware of the feelings of others. They understand that everyone is special. When we were using, we probably didn't have the time or energy to be kind or to even notice the kindness in others. It is hard to be kind when we're running from ourselves.

Now we can look around us and see the kindness in others. We can find people who will help us feel special. Most of all, today we can be kind. We can help others feel special. By giving kindness we open ourselves to receiving it. When we give kindness, it spreads out naturally, and multiplies. In this way, we change our world with a small act.

Today let me remember to be kind and loving.

One day at a time—this is enough. Live in the present and make it so beautiful that it will be worth remembering.

Ida Scott Taylor

Today is our most important day. Today is what counts—not yesterday, not tomorrow. It doesn't matter if we've been sober for three years or two days. It doesn't matter if we did something terrible yesterday, or if we plan to do something terrific tomorrow.

In recovery, every day is a time to take inventory and change our lives in some way. Every day gives us the chance to start over. We can share our experience, strength, and hope with a new person in recovery. We can start developing our talents. With God's help, every day can be the start of a great new life.

Today let me grow in a new way and be grateful for it.

June 20

*I struggle so hard to be accepted
by people that I forget how to
relax and be myself.*

Joseph Morgan

Most of us honor and respect people who love themselves enough to be themselves. We can learn that art, too, when we stop trying to please everyone. Instead of wanting to be loved, we can try loving. Instead of thinking only of our own needs, we can recognize the pain of someone else. When we stop thinking about our own needs and feelings, we often are more attractive to others, too.

Wisdom is practicing the art of seeing ourselves as part of instead of apart from others. Instead of focusing on the pain of rejection, we can focus on what we have to give others.

Today let me believe in myself and know that I am lovable.

*We are all dependent on one
another, every soul of us on earth.*

George Bernard Shaw

In order to get well, we have to admit that we alone are powerless over our disease. We need other people to help us.

This is hard for us to do. We aren't used to needing anyone or asking for help. We all pushed people away after we started using.

We know now that our way never worked, and that we need help. There will always be someone who will help lead us along the path toward the sobriety and serenity we want. But to ask for this help takes both courage and humility. We gain support from this risk, and also new strength, fellowship, and wisdom. Each time we take the chance to ask for help, we are exercising control over our lives.

Today let me remember I am not alone by asking another for something I need.

June 22

*A ship in harbor is safe, but that
is not what ships are built for.*

William Shedd

Recovery asks us to put ourselves on the
line. Who are we really? What are our
deepest dreams, secrets, and fears? We feel
happiest after we've turned and faced our
personal monsters. Facing us now is the risk
that brings freedom. We need to let someone
know about all of us—with no reservations.
Our shame blocks our progress when it says
we've done, thought, or said things too bad to
tell anyone. This can keep us stuck sitting on
the sidelines of our own lives.

We are ships ready to leave the harbor.
We are our own best life companions. We
deserve to love ourselves for exactly who we
are.

*Today let me risk loving and sharing the real
me.*

Enjoyment is not a goal, it is a feeling that accompanies important ongoing activity.

Paul Goodman

When we first get into recovery, many of us are afraid we'll never enjoy anything again. How will we have a good time if we aren't using? It doesn't seem fun; it seems boring.

Our lives may have been chaotic and totally unmanageable before, but at least they were exciting. Now things are predictable. And it seems a little dull.

Our bodies and our emotions are healing. We can be sure, though, as time passes, we will be enjoying normal, everyday things more and more. This process never stops as long as we are recovering. As we take care of ourselves, we get better than we ever were.

Today let me appreciate the fun of some small, healthy exercise.

*The feeling that will never come
back anymore. The feeling that I
could last forever, outlast the sea,
the earth, all men.*

Joseph Conrad

Some days our energy feels like a live
thing inside us. We have so much energy we
feel as if we might break open.

Addiction took all our time and thoughts,
and used up all our energy. In recovery, we
often have a new surge of energy that's so
good it's almost scary. We may worry that
we're not used to feeling so alive. It's new to
us. But with help from others and our program, we soon learn our new zest for life can
be channeled into recovery. We are not out of
control, we are simply bursting with new life.
We can learn to trust these good feelings as we
learn to recover from our addiction.

*Today let me accept the strong feelings of my
youth.*

*I will really be free. . .when I
learn to speak up for me without
harming thee.*

Sue Stenberg

Being assertive means sharing honestly
how we feel and asking for what we need,
without putting the other person down. When
we're aggressive, we demand and bully others
to get what we want and need.

When we're assertive we simply say what
we feel and what we need. This honest, open
sharing of our deepest feelings can be scary at
first. We don't have the armor of anger to
protect us. But as we practice being assertive, we find it comes easier. And we can take
new pride in being able to get our needs met
without hurting others. We find that being
assertive gives us real power.

*Today let me have the honesty to examine the
way I come across to others.*

*Our patience will achieve more
than our force.*

Edmund Burke

Patience is something many of us don't
have. We were used to immediate highs. Now
we have a lot to learn about patience.

At first we're just impatient to get better.
When will we have the serenity we see in
other people? We want our families to trust
us now. We want new friendships now; we
want serenity and happiness today.

Usually when we're impatient it's because we're trying to do things our way. We
aren't trusting our Higher Power. But by saying "God, You do what you want in my life,"
things get better. We start feeling more
content, more willing to do the work it takes
to change our lives. We become more patient.
We realize our lives are being slowly trans-
formed, one day at a time.

Today let me let God work in my life.

*God is our refuge and strength, a
very present help in trouble.*

Psalms 46:1

We're all afraid of something, whether it's
something we need to do at work or school, or
something we need to say to someone. We can
release our fear by remembering to "let go and
let God." We can prepare ourselves as well as
we can, and then let our Higher Power handle
the rest. Sometimes despite all our prayers,
we keep taking back our fears. For those
times, we can use a God box. It can be any size
or shape. The point is that anything that goes
in the box has been given to God. When we are
worried about something, we can put it in our
God box, and ask God to help us with it.

We may doubt that writing things down
and putting them in a box helps, but it often
does. This is the work of a Higher Power.

*Today let me turn over the things I need help
with.*

June 28

Water is the only drink for a wise man.

Henry David Thoreau

When we were using, we didn't feel our feelings. The drugs altered what we felt. Now, when we're abstinent, we start to feel normal feelings again and this might come as a shock. The new feelings will seem to be very strong and powerful, and we may think they can't be normal. They are normal. After a while we get used to feeling again and don't feel as raw or intense. Soon, we'll start to feel things the way others do and eventually we'll get used to it and enjoy it. Abstinence is making our heads grow clearer. At first the clear-headedness will feel uncomfortable, but later it will feel normal and natural.

Today let me be joyful that I'm thinking and feeling more clearly all the time.

*How shall we expect charity
towards others, when we are
uncharitable to ourselves?*

Sir Thomas Browne

Many of us suffer from low self-esteem.
We didn't like ourselves to begin with, and it
got worse after we started using. Now that
we're in recovery, feeling good about ourselves still doesn't come easily. We remember
the things we did when we were using, the
things we did that were against our values.

When we are burdened with these
thoughts, we can simply admit those acts to
our Higher Power and to ourselves. And then
we find another human being we feel safe
enough with to share the things that keep us
feeling bad about ourselves. By doing this, we
learn we are not bad people. We just did bad
things when we were caught up in an illness
that is much bigger than we are.

Today help me share with someone I trust.

June 30

The ability to accept responsibility is the measure of the man.

Roy L. Smith

We are stricken by a disease. However, we can be grateful that our disease is treatable. A cancer victim may have different treatment options to choose from and there are no guarantees. A victim of addiction has one option for getting well—sobriety. As soon as we get sober, we are no longer victims. We are active participants in the guarantee of recovery. We can shake off the victim feeling and begin realizing we shape our own future.

Today we can remind ourselves that we are not victims anymore. We have been given a disease with a hidden gift. In recovery from addiction, we can actually be far more healthy than we were before we suffered from the disease. We can rise up and succeed.

Today let me say goodbye to the victim in me and hello to the winner in me.

*Love alone is capable of uniting
living beings in such a way as to
complete and fulfill them, for it
alone takes them and joins them
by what is deepest in themselves.*

Pierre T. De Chardin

There is a part of us that longs to be shared with another human being. It feels wonderful when someone else's heart touches ours. It is wonderful to be loved.

We have filled our hearts up with searchings, feelings, and memories. This is who we really are. It is the only gift we can bring to someone else.

The best kind of love listens without judging or criticizing. The best kind of love gently walks through the garbage of our past looking for roses. We are all beautiful inside and love finds our beauty instead of our faults.

Today let me find the roses in the lives of those I love.

July 2

In bringing up children, spend
on them half as much money
and twice as much time.

Laurence J. Peter

Sometimes we feel like commercials on TV when we're with our families. We get listened to and glanced at between the important programs. They seem like they are always on the run. If they really liked us, wouldn't they have more time for us? Often, we don't know if it's really time we want. We mostly want to feel important to them.

It's easy to feel resentment toward our parents, but feeling resentment is a luxury we can't afford. We are well enough now to realize that our parents may also have been terribly hurt, and to take the risk to ask for special individual time with them.

Today let me have the courage to ask for what I need.

*One's friends are that part of the
human race with which one can
be human.*

George Santayana

We sometimes have friends who criticize
us. These friendships are confusing because
these people can also be very nice to us. After
a while, these friendships can become very
sad because the regular criticism hurts.

We know now that we don't have to let
people hurt us. Some of our friends weren't
really friends at all. They just needed someone to feel superior to. Others are really
friends who are trying to help, but don't realize how much they are hurting us.

Today we can leave behind the superior
ones and let the others know how we really
feel. Our true friends will understand and be
supportive.

*Today let me be a true friend and have a true
friend.*

July 4

Roads go ever, ever on
Under cloud and under star,
Yet feet that wandering have gone
Turn at last to home afar.

J. R. R. Tolkien

Holidays can be difficult times. No matter how old we get, we seem to expect to be happy on holidays. Getting high on expectations can bring disaster. Going home for a holiday can be emotionally jarring especially if our families are not perfect.

We can start feeling good about holidays by remembering that neither a person or a family can be perfect. Starting with this thought makes it possible for holidays to become very special loving times. If we focus on what we can give instead of what we're getting, we can feel good about holidays.

Today let me enjoy my family for what it is instead of what I want it to be.

*Every man passes his life in
search after friendship.*

                    Ralph Waldo Emerson

Being sober isn't easy at first. When we first sober up, it seems like we don't have any friends at all. Others who have always been sober aren't too sure about us. And we know we can't hang around with the friends we used to use with. It seems lonely at first.

That's when we have to trust our Higher Power that things will get better and little by little, they do. Gradually we make new friends who accept us as the clean and sober people we now are. In the end, we have friends we care about, friends who really care about us, more friends than we ever had when we were using. These friendships are deep, supportive, honest, and lasting. It takes a little time, but it's worth it.

Today help me make one new friend.

July 6

*Let us not burden our remem-
brances with a heaviness that is
gone.*

William Shakespeare

Anger is sometimes called the out-of-
control emotion. It has the reputation for
being the most dangerous emotion. And yet,
it's also a healthy, normal feeling as well. It's
not that anger is bad, but if we are angry and
don't do anything about it, it can hurt us.

Anger is a part of us, just as love, fear, and
courage are. There is nothing unhealthy
about feeling angry—it is our radar. Anger
can let us know when we're being mistreated.
Unexpressed anger, though, can lead to depression, and can clog our lives with feelings
from the past that may not apply to the
present. When we truly live in the present,
our anger acts as one of the guides by which
we know ourselves and others know us.

Today let me recognize my anger.

. . . when a man loves, he seeks no power, and therefore he has power.

Alan Paton

True power comes from love that is trusting and uncontrolling. When we try to possess and guard another person, we become their jailers. It is the nature of man to want to escape from jail. True love allows a partner the freedom to grow. Insecure people don't believe that they're lovable, so they sometimes use their power to try and control their partner.

Our challenge is to find a new way to relate in openly loving systems. We know that love and control are not the same. Today we can love without controlling.

Today let me appreciate the freedom that true love allows.

July 8

Never build a case against yourself.

Norman Vincent Peale

Sometimes because of our fear of failure, we built a case against ourselves. In the past, we often became so discouraged and down on ourselves that we lost energy. This negativity seemed to breed more negativity and before long we stopped worrying about failing. We just stopped trying.

We are lucky today. We know how bad it feels to be negative, but we also know how to change the negatives into positives. We have friends and a fellowship that have taught us how good we really are, how alive we can be, and how to look forward to a bright tomorrow.

Today let me build a positive case for myself.

*Complaint is the largest tribute
Heaven receives, and the sincerest
part of our devotion.*

Jonathan Swift

God can handle all our complaints, worries, and problems. God has wide shoulders and it's His job to carry us and all our problems. We needn't feel guilty because we complain to God. There is no magic or right way to pray. When we pray, it is the time we can truly be ourselves—good and bad. God doesn't judge our prayer. He's just glad we are sharing with Him what we really feel.

God has all the time in the world just for us. Sometimes we might not want to burden God because we think our problems are too small. There is no problem too small or too big for God to handle.

Today let me ask God, without hesitation, for what I need.

July 10

*I've been in so many quickie
relationships that emotionally I
felt like a piece of Swiss cheese.*

Julie Reinhardts

Sometimes our need to be loved feels so big that we accept abusive behavior from others. We wonder who we really are. Drifting from one relationship to another, we keep hoping that the next one will be better. They usually get worse instead of better. We allow ourselves to be sexually, verbally, and emotionally used and abused.

Living in an abuse cycle is slow death. We don't have to live this way any longer. We can learn to take good care of ourselves and we have the right to be respected. With the help of others, we can begin to heal. We can open up and get honest with a safe, caring person to begin the healing process.

Today let me begin my journey back to myself.

*God grant me the serenity to
accept the things I cannot change,
courage to change the things I
can, and wisdom to know the difference.*

The Serenity Prayer

The principles of our program of recovery
help us with everything in our lives. We can
use the Serenity Prayer every day to keep us
from getting too upset about anything. Saying the Serenity Prayer helps us preserve our
serenity enough to move on with our lives.

"One day at a time" reminds us to tell
ourselves that we only have to do what we can
today, and tomorrow will take care of itself.
And "Easy does it" helps us to keep from getting mad about things.

We have a new life now, one that requires
our full attention and rewards us with serenity, friends, self-respect, and growth.

Today let me remember that "Easy does it."

July 12

It is easier to stay out than get out.

Mark Twain

In the program we are told to stay out of slippery places if we don't want to slip. Perhaps at first we didn't believe that was necessary. Maybe it didn't seem fair for people to tell us to stay away from friends we had known for so long. When we feel this way, we need to remember how much trouble alcohol and drugs caused in our lives.

We have a new life now, and there is no room in it for old ways of doing things. When we start minimizing the problems we had when we were using, we need to call someone for help. This is why today we surround ourselves with new friends, people who are serious about staying clean and sober. These are the people who really care. Why cheat ourselves out of their help?

Today let me stay out of slippery places.

*We know what we are, but know
not what we may be.*

William Shakespeare

When we first start recovering, staying
sober is our only goal. After a while, being
clean and sober is simply our new way of life.
Then we find there are a lot of questions about
the future we face. We need to start thinking
about these things.

What should we do with the future? There
are some things we can do that help. We can
pay attention to the types of things we like to
do today. We can try to visualize what a
certain career would be like.

Sometimes we just need to turn the whole
matter over to our Higher Power. It's nice to
know that trusting God works with other
decisions, just like it does with staying sober.

*Today let me have faith that things will work
out the best for me.*

July 14

Winter, spring, summer or fall ...
you've got a friend.

      Carole King

What a great feeling it is to know we can make friends. Once, we had little or no idea what a friend really was. We used people and they used us. Now we know that using isn't friendship.

True friendship is such a relief. We can be ourselves. We can say what we like and what we don't like. We don't have to pretend to be someone we're not. Our friends today love and accept us for who we are—warts and all.

The best part of discovering true friendship is the joy we feel in giving and in being a true friend ourselves. We give love and respect to our friends. They return love and respect. We are at peace with the world.

Today let me cherish my ability to be a friend and to have a friend.

*Human service is the highest
form of self-interest for the person
who serves.*

Elbert Hubbard

Doing something for others can be healing, both for us and for them. In recovery, we have to help one another in order to stay sober. This helps us keep things in perspective. The strange thing about helping someone else is that we often come back to our own problems with new wisdom and find the answers easily. Sometimes our Higher Power has taken care of our problems while we were helping someone else .

When we keep in mind that we are helping others in order to help ourselves, when we remember to keep working on our own problems while offering this help, we grow stronger and wiser.

Today let me be available to help someone else in some way.

*. . . once you are REAL you can't
be ugly, except to people who don't
understand.*

Margery Williams

Real beauty shines from the inside out.
We can't all be the handsomest boy or the
most beautiful girl in school. We can, though,
be beautiful people all the same. We can be
honest, caring, and thoughtful. We can find a
healthy way to serve others and ourselves.
We can develop our spiritual lives and find
more conscious contact with our Higher Power.
We can learn to love and accept ourselves and
others as they are, without conditions. Then,
we will be beautiful no matter what our faces
or bodies look like.

Beauty is something that comes from
inside. We can all be beautiful.

*Today let honesty, love, and caring shine
through me.*

*There is in each of us so much
goodness that if we could see its
glow, it would light the world.*

Sam Friend

We are starting to believe in the goodness
of our spirits. We are beginning to feel the
steady warmth of an inner flame that won't go
out. We are claiming the goodness in ourselves.

Sometimes we do make poor decisions,
but we are learning from them. It's hard for
many of us to claim and accept goodness as
our own because we are so used to emotionally
beating ourselves.

We are challenged in recovery to accept
and love the best in ourselves and to let go of
old negative thinking. It is true that God
loves us unconditionally.

Today let me accept my deep down goodness.

July 18

*God will be present whether
asked or not.*

Latin Proverb

Many of us had a hard time at first turning our lives over to a Higher Power. We were so used to having things our way. We knew we needed help with our addiction, but turning everything over to God seemed pretty drastic. We may have had a hard time believing His will for us might be just as good, or even better, than our will for ourselves. But as we looked at our past, we realized that pursuing our will hadn't made us happy. Sometimes we made ourselves miserable trying to force things to happen.

Little by little, we are turning different parts of our lives over to God. Life is smoother, we are happier and more serene. From these experiences, our trust increases daily.

Today let me turn one part of my life over to my Higher Power.

We do not see nature with our eyes, but with our understanding and our hearts.

William Hazlitt

One way to contact our Higher Power is in nature. In winter, we can feel the chill in the air, and the warmth deep inside us. In spring we can delight in everything coming alive again. In summer, we love the freedom we feel. In fall, the turning of the leaves reminds us of the passage of time.

We can find peace outdoors. The hustle and bustle of life slows down as we sink into the eternity of nature. We are reminded that we are not the center of the universe.

At times it almost seems like God speaks to us outdoors. These times spent outdoors alone with nature give us fresh air for the body, mind, and spirit.

Today let me take time to find my place in nature.

Peace is a daily, a weekly, a monthly process, gradually changing opinions, slowly eroding old barriers, quietly building new structures.

John F. Kennedy

After we began to recover, we may have expected our lives to be problem-free. Once we stopped using, we may have thought there would never be any more conflict.

It isn't that easy. We still may have arguments about things we're doing. We may still disagree with our families. We may still find ourselves in conflict from time to time.

At times like these, we can remind ourselves we're the only one we can change. We can use what we've learned in recovery to help us. The more we do this, the easier it gets, and the more peaceful our lives become.

Today let me do one thing to eliminate a conflict.

Worry gives a small thing a big shadow.

Swedish Proverb

Before we got into recovery, we used to worry about everything. We acted like nothing worried us, but underneath, a lot did. We worried about being caught using; we worried about what people thought of us; we worried about how we'd end up if we kept drinking and drugging. We found that if we got high again, those worries disappeared for a while.

Now we've learned there is another way to live. We can live one day at a time and do our best in that twenty-four-hour period. And when we do worry about things sometimes, we can use the tools of the program: call our sponsor, talk to our other friends, go to more meetings, or pray. When we do those things, the worries disappear.

Today let me ask for help with what I'm worried about.

July 22

*I know the grass beyond the door,
the sweet keen smell.*

Dante Gabriel Rossetti

There is a tale about a king who wanted only the wisest man to be his prime minister. When the search narrowed down to three men, he put them to a test. He placed them in a room and installed an impressive lock on the door. Whoever was able to leave the room would be prime minister.

Two began to work out complicated schemes to get out. The third sat and thought. Finally, the third man walked to the door and turned the handle. The door had been unlocked all the time.

Sometimes we complicate a simple program and don't trust that recovery is there for us. The door of recovery is unlocked, and all we have to do is turn the handle to enter into a new and joyous life.

Today let me be willing to open the door.

*Out of the depths have I cried
unto thee, O Lord.*

Psalms 130:1

We all need to recover from something.
For some of us, that recovery is from drugs or
alcohol. For others, the recovery might be
from an unhappy or abusive childhood. Or
perhaps, we have lost a loved one. No one
really makes it through life without some
hardship. The trick is not to drown in the
hardship.

We can recover from whatever happens to
us. We might fall several times along the path
to recovery, but with God's help, we can go on.

People alone are fighters. Fighters who
use God's help are survivors. We can win
today. We can be sure that nothing is too big,
with the help of God, to handle.

*Today let me reach for the lifesaver of God's
help.*

*The greatest pleasure I know is to
do a good action by stealth, and
to have it found out by accident.*

Charles Lamb

When we were using, we did a lot of the
taking in life. We took people's trust, gener-
osity, and efforts to help us. Now that we're
getting healthy, we can be givers.

Giving makes us feel good. Saving money
and buying a special surprise for a friend feels
terrific. Seeing their look of happiness warms
the heart.

Sometimes it feels good to tell people
about the good things we've done. Other
times, it feels terrific to keep our good deeds a
secret and just let people be surprised. Either
way, giving almost always feels better than
taking. Now we can know the joy of giving.
We can look forward to the opportunity to
give.

Today I will give of myself.

*The first problem for all of us,
men and women, is not to learn,
but to unlearn.*

Gloria Steinem

Using was a way of life. Being clean and sober is another, completely different way of life. Everything must be unlearned and replaced with the attitudes and behaviors of a new lifestyle. Old friends must be left for new, healthy ones. What we choose to say and even to think must be unlearned and replaced.

We are lucky in a way. We get the chance to change our lives around at a time when many of our friends are settling into lifetime routines. Many of them are standing still, but we get to move forward with new, exciting lives.

Today I choose recovery and a new life.

*Respect yourself if you would
have others respect you.*

Baltasar Gracián

When we were using, a lot of us had a low opinion of ourselves, and the people around us reinforced it. Our parents told us how much trouble we caused. Our teachers or employers told us we didn't live up to our potential.

Now that we are in recovery, we are building our self-esteem. Every day that we stay clean and sober, we feel better about ourselves. We know we are becoming the kind of people we admire.

The people around us are starting to admire us again. It doesn't happen over night, but the people around us do respond to the change. Feeling good about ourselves is one of the best parts of being in recovery.

Today help me see how much I've changed for the better.

*We can bear the loss of love for
only one day at a time.*

Sam Friend

All of us have experienced the pain and
loss of a broken relationship. We know the
feeling of aloneness when someone we counted
on and loved is no longer in our lives. We
sometimes feel that the pain is too much to
bear. We wonder how we can go on without
this person in our lives. Looking past today
into our entire lifetime is something we do
regularly and something that can be very
frightening.

We know now that we don't have to cope
with loss for an entire lifetime. Our lifetime
only really happens to us one day at a time. So
the loss we feel only has to be dealt with one
day at a time. This we can handle. Today we
can deal with what happens to us. We can
look forward to tomorrow with courage.

Today let me deal only with today.

July 28

*I care not so much what I am in
the opinion of others, as what I
am in my own.*

Montaigne

We often think that our families and friends will recover just because we are. Then we find out that they are not as thrilled about our recovery as we think they should be. Sometimes they become very uncomfortable with us. This discomfort will probably show up in how they relate to us. They may react with anger. They may totally withdraw from us or ridicule us for joining the program.

We can stay sober no matter what other people's reaction is to us. They must live their lives, and we must let go of trying to control them. The only thing we can have power over is this moment in our own lives. By staying sober, we take steps each moment to a better life.

Today let me remember whose life I am living.

*Never does the human soul
appear so strong as when it
forgoes revenge, and dares forgive
an injury.*

E. H. Chapin

When something or someone makes us angry and we deny it or ignore it, the anger can become a resentment. Resentments hurt us because they make us suffer. They make us angry, negative, and short-tempered.

The key to preventing resentments is to start expressing our feelings either verbally or in writing. We do this not to change the other person, but to unload from ourselves the poison of resentment. We can let go of it. We can be grateful that as we empty ourselves of negative things, the space will be filled with positives.

Today let me express my feelings in a way that feels safe and then turn them over to my Higher Power.

*The most common sort of lie is the
one uttered to one's self.*

       Friedrich Nietzsche

Once in a while, when our denial starts up again, we may wonder if we're really addicted. When this happens, we need to remember that we already tried to be social users. We tried drinking just a little bit or using just a little drugs, but we weren't successful. We can remember all the trouble, all the lies, and the hopelessness of feeling we'd never be able to stop.

We can be grateful for those memories now, because they remind us we really are powerless over alcohol and drugs. We are getting our physical health back. And spiritually and emotionally, recovery can help us become better than we were before we started using.

Today let me remember I am powerless over my addiction.

*I felt lifted up, as though the
great clean wind of a mountain
top blew through and through.*

Bill Wilson

We each have our own spiritual experiences. Sometimes they are small, quiet happenings that we hardly notice, but can feel deep down in our souls. Other times they are explosive realizations that change our lives. All of them are miracles.

At one time, we never would have noticed these wonderful experiences. Now we can get quiet and look into our souls and marvel at what is happening there. We are spiritual as well as physical beings. Our physical side used to dominate us and keep us from getting to know the spiritual. Now we can learn to know and appreciate every part of our beings. This is the miracle of our lives.

Today let me be open to the daily miracles in my life.

August 1

It is manlike to punish but
godlike to forgive.

Peter VonWinter

When we forgive, we don't always forget. Sometimes it takes a great deal of time to forget painful hurts. Being human, we feel anger. The challenge of recovery is to learn a direct and honest way to express our anger. When we hold onto anger, it turns into resentment. The word resentment actually means to "refeel." When we refeel old hurts, we become poisoned and hurt ourselves.

Forgiveness is a process that doesn't happen overnight. Forgiveness means that we are willing to let go of rethinking and refeeling old hurts. At first, this may be hard because angry energy pops up again and again. Now we are learning to pray and let go of these negative feelings.

Today let me have the willingness to let go of resentment.

*It can be no dishonor to learn
from others when they speak good
sense.*

Sophocles

Being young and in recovery wasn't easy at first. Some of us found few people our age in meetings. Many of us didn't like this.

But when we started listening to what the older people were saying in meetings, our attitudes changed. Their stories were different from ours, but they were similar, too.

Once we let down our guard and accept the older members of the group, we can see that age doesn't matter—we are all recovering from the same disease. Our advantage is being able to hear the advice and wisdom of elders who have been where we are, and who are enjoying the fruits of recovery that we want, too.

Today let me listen to the advice of someone older and wiser.

August 3

Genuine love cannot endure silence. Genuine love breaks out into speech.

Myles Connolly

Today we can risk saying, "I love you" to others. We used to feel frightened to open our hearts to people. We never believed we were worthwhile people. We needed love so badly. We put on a tough front and were afraid to ask for what we needed. We built such a strong wall that people were afraid of us. But then we began to earn self-respect, and self-love, again. We began to realize we are on a search for self-fulfillment, not perfection. We found we are able to drop the tough front with others. We are able to be touched with love.

We begin to trust that we aren't so bad, we can reach out to others and share our real feelings. The amazing thing is that people will love us back.

Today let me celebrate life and love.

*God enters by a private door into
every individual.*

Ralph Waldo Emerson

Some days it feels like the program isn't
working for us anymore. We're still going to
meetings, but we don't seem to be getting
much out of them. What's wrong? Well,
maybe we aren't using all the tools of the
program. By using the tools of the program,
we are turning our lives and will over to our
Higher Power.

We can't recover in a day. It is a life-long
journey, and there will be other times when
we'll feel this way. Everyone has down times.
Not everyone knows what we know—that we
have the tools to work our way out of them. In
recovery, our lives are filled with power—the
power of a Higher Power Whom we have
turned things over to, and our own power to
take action to get ourselves back on track.

Today let me ask for help and accept it.

August 5

*Understanding is a two-way
street.*

Eleanor Roosevelt

It is often frustrating when people around us don't understand our new way of life. Sometimes people don't understand our need to go to meetings. Other times families think they can keep us sober. They watch our every move, trying to protect us from things they think will influence us to use again.

We can share with them our understanding of addiction. We can explain that regular meetings are as close to a cure as we can get, that the urge to use can return at any time if we aren't working our program. We can explain that our sobriety is our responsibility, not theirs.

Finally, we can be as understanding of their fears as we want them to be of our recovery.

Today let me help a loved one understand.

*That man's silence is wonderful
to listen to.*

Thomas Hardy

Sometimes we learn more about someone by hearing what they don't say rather than what they do say. If a girl screams, "I'm so mad at you!" and she has tears rolling down her cheeks, she's saying something. Probably she's really more hurt than mad. We often have trouble telling our true feelings. Telling someone they hurt us is admitting we can be hurt.

When we learn to trust ourselves and others, we can talk freely about our feelings. We find we can trust without fear. We begin to learn that people can only be careful of us when they know who we really are. And we can be more loving toward ourselves, too.

Today let me pay attention to what I am really saying, and what people are really trying to tell me.

August 7

My strength is made perfect in weakness.

II Corinthians 12:9

If we don't think we're powerless, we're in danger of using again. We have to be honest about the fact that our lives did not work when we were drinking and drugging.

By admitting our powerlessness, we give ourselves back all the energy and strength it once took to try to control our addiction and to keep our secret. With this strength, and the help of our Higher Power and our sober friends, we are stronger than ever. But we are only strong as long as we admit our complete weakness over our addiction. Knowing this, we can use our strength to get better, to take risks and share ourselves, and to see that we too deserve happiness.

Today let me admit my powerlessness over addiction and use my strength in recovery.

*Faith is to believe what we do not
see; and the reward of this faith is
to see what we believe.*

St. Augustine

Very few of us believed we could ever be
sane again. Even those of us who believed in
God didn't see how He could help. Perhaps we
had gone to church from time to time, thinking that would stop our drinking and drugging, but it didn't—at least not for very long.

We will come to understand how our
Higher Power is healing us. It will happen as
we go to meetings regularly, as we listen to
other people's stories, as we realize the healing that has taken place in them. We will
come to believe it is possible for us, too.

When we know it is possible, it is already
beginning. When we can see it happening—
bit by bit—we are looking in the right places
for the treasure that is our lives.

Today let me feel my Higher Power in my life.

August 9

*I must love the questions them-
selves. . .like locked rooms, full of
treasures to which my blind and
groping key does not yet fit.*

Alice Walker

Learning to love our own problems and
questions may sound crazy, but it's true. Life
used to feel like a speeding train. We liked the
thrill of the ride but the crashes started to
hurt too much.

Recovery is discovery. We are asking new
questions of life, and discovering the locked
rooms of wonderful treasures we carry inside.
As we rediscover ourselves, we learn all over
again how to love and accept ourselves. And
we begin to find joy in the act of discovery
itself. Recovery is an adventure.

*Today let me be a prospector in the gold fields
of my own life.*

*Just get it down on paper, and
then we'll see what to do with it.*

Maxwell Perkins

Our memories are tricky things. We remember the critical things people say more than the compliments. We may forget how badly we felt a year or a week ago. It can help to keep a diary, even if we only write a few lines each day. We can write down how we feel at the moment. Then if we're feeling like we haven't made progress, we can look through the diary and realize how far we've come.

When we're worried about something, it helps to put it down on paper. We can ask ourselves if we're working our program around this issue, and write down how we're doing it. Once we see things written down, they seem more clear, and it's easier to see what we need to do to get back on track.

Today let me take the time to write down how I feel.

August 11

*If I knew what I was so anxious
about, I wouldn't be so anxious.*

Mignon McLaughlin

Knowledge is power, especially self-knowledge. Somehow, the things that stay locked inside us hurt us the most. The little worries and anxieties of life can drain our time and fill our lives with uncertainty.

There is a lot we can do to relieve the tension and worry in our lives today. We know that we are powerless to change other people, places, and things but we can change ourselves. We can change our worrying attitude by really believing we have the resources to make our lives better. We can stop worrying and start living.

Today let me stop worrying about things I can't change.

*My sweet Lord. I really want to
know You.*

George Harrison

Do we believe that God is our true friend?
Do we believe that God is always there just for
us? Do we believe that God is protecting us
even when we don't ask Him to?

God doesn't take holidays, naps, or time
off. He is on twenty-four-hour call, and His
line is never busy. God is the original positive
person. He always wants us to be happy, and
understands us when we're not. Imagine all
of the love for all time filling our whole planet.
That love is just one tiny drop in the bucket of
what God feels for each one of us.

Do we deserve so much love? We don't
have to deserve God's love. It's a gift that
never leaves. We can make a call to God
today. The lines are not busy.

Today let me talk to my Higher Power.

August 13

*You grow up the day you have
your first real laugh at yourself.*

Edith Barrymore

In recovery, we learn to forgive ourselves and laugh at what we did before, instead of hurting. Now we've been given the gift of life, and we're smiling a lot more. We find we can laugh at the world, at each other, and even at ourselves. We can decide to hang on to unpleasant feelings, or we can let them go like a puff of dandelion fluff.

In life, we choose which side of the fence to fall on. Addiction is serious business and usually turns people into pretty serious folks. Recovery helps us to find humor again. It helps us to laugh and giggle, and in doing so, cleanse ourselves and lighten the load.

Today let me learn to laugh at myself.

*For time will teach thee soon the
truth. There are no birds in last
year's nest!*

Henry W. Longfellow

This moment is the only moment we have.
Our yesterdays are memories and our tomorrows are uncertain dreams. This moment is
life's best gift to us. We are given two things
to work with today. We are given this day in
time and the power over our own attitude. We
are the only ones who can make or break this
day. Do we really believe that what goes on in
this day will make our life stories? It does, so
we better not spend too much time today
feeling bad about our past or worrying about
our future.

We can learn to live in the now instead of
the past or the future. Each day is a gift, to be
treasured. Each day is a chance to start all
over again, growing in love and serenity.

*Today let me cherish the moment and learn to
live in the now.*

August 15

*I am only one, but still I am one.
I cannot do everything, but still I
can do something. I will not
refuse to do the something I can
do.*

Helen Keller

Sometimes we pick up the wrong yard-stick when measuring our self-worth. If we come up short, we think we're worthless.

We all have things we do well, and things we don't do well. Being the best isn't nearly as important as trying our best. Sometimes we do things better than a lot of other people. Other times we don't do very well at all. We can't afford to let either of these get to us. We are neither our successes nor our failures. We are a combination of both.

Today, we can forgive ourselves and try to do better next time. We can love ourselves for our courage, our strength, and our successes.

Let me be willing to do the best that I can.

*There are too many people, and
too few human beings.*

Robert Zend

We all have some difficult people in our
lives. We sometimes feel these people are
asking us to prove something to them. We
often feel that we will never measure up in
their eyes, that we will never be able to do
enough. We are growing people with weaknesses and will sometimes disappoint the
people we love. We wonder why we feel so
hurt and defensive when someone tells us
that we haven't loved them well enough.

We know today that we don't have to
prove anything to anyone but ourselves. We
know now that we can't please everyone all
the time and that we don't even have to try.
We can choose today who we want to please
and why.

*Today let me remain emotionally detached
from difficult people.*

*In any relationship in which two
people become one, the end result
is two half people.*

Dr. Wayne Dyer

Relationships can be scary. We used to
get high in order to date. Sometimes all our
insecurities came out in the dating situation.
We met someone we liked and we felt good
inside. Being addicts, we wanted to increase
the good feelings and ensure that we would
have that person forever. Instead of talking
about our fears, we often panicked and tried
to possess the person.

Today we have the courage to take an
honest look at our relationships. If necessary,
we can let go of harmful relationships. Getting honest about relationships is the beginning of real emotional recovery. And we know
now that what we want most is recovery.

*Today let me be honest about my relation-
ships.*

The weak can never forgive.
Forgiveness is the attribute of the
strong.

Mahatma Gandhi

When we're confronted by a foe, we should praise him, bless him, and let him go. Holding on to anger is like adding wood to a slow burning fire. The longer the fire burns, the more pain it causes us and others.

When we try to get even with someone, we are like soldiers in a war with no ending. Hurting the other person doesn't stop our struggle, it just adds more wood to the fire.

Sometimes we might need to swallow our pride and retreat from the battle. What would it mean for us to practice not having the last word? It would mean peace. We give ourselves freedom the minute we are able to let go of resentments. When the last words are "I forgive," we can get on with our lives.

Today let me have the courage to forgive.

August 19

Some people, no matter how old
they get, never lose their beauty.
They merely move it from their
faces into their hearts.

Martin Buxbaum

Some days we feel obsessed with looking
good. We don't even want to go out if our hair
and clothes aren't perfect. Some days one
pimple feels like a thousand. Why do we feel
that physical appearance is so important? We
compare ourselves to others and usually come
up short. Most of us can accept imperfection
in our friends a lot easier than we accept it for
ourselves. We are our own worst critics.

We can begin to realize our own beauty
and learn to love ourselves as we are. Instead
of demanding perfection, let's celebrate ourselves as children of God, human and growing.

Today let me select one thing I like about
myself and remember it, no matter what.

*He who can have patience can
have what he will.*

Benjamin Franklin

Patience meant waiting, and waiting wasn't something we were good at. Growing up was hard for us because when we wanted something, we wanted it now. We would get frustrated and become demanding. We used to get our way by acting angry.

Now we can see that impatience and anger were ways we manipulated people. Our anger gave us a false sense of power, but on the inside we were scared little kids who didn't know how to play by the rules of life.

Today we are learning that patience and tolerance can make us winners. We are slowly learning that being the center of the universe is a lonely and sad place to be. We are also learning that learning patience takes patience, but the payoff is a whole new life to enjoy.

Today let me practice patience.

August 21

*Forgiveness is the answer to the
child's dream of a miracle of
which what is broken is made
whole again, what is soiled is
again made clean.*

Dag Hammarskjöld

Sometimes we feel afraid of the strong
feelings we have. These feelings can erupt at
any time. Sometimes we are ashamed of ourselves because of our feelings. Shame is like
a snake in the process of recovery.

Recovery teaches us to face our feelings
and our past. First, we need to talk about our
concerns with someone we trust. We do this
to expose and heal our shames and fears.
Recovery is learning to take responsibility in
making healthy decisions and learning to accept our humanness as we honestly explore
our histories.

*Today help me forgive myself for something I
did while actively addicted.*

*There is a magic, beauty, and
grandeur in reaching the top of
our personal mountain of physical gifts.*

Jackson Browne

Sports are a wonderful release and relief
from our everyday worries and cares. Using
our muscles, wits, and intelligence, we feel
whole. It is great to feel that good tennis serve
happen or to experience the thrill of a perfect
throw to first base. There is a magic moment
for a swimmer when the breathing falls into
balance.

Strength, motion, and grace meet to make
those special moments in sports that are
difficult to feel any other way. Even if our only
sport is riding a bike or roller skating, when
we are doing it right, we are confident, powerful, in balance, and getting better all the time.

*Today let me work at something athletic and
try to find a sport just for me.*

August 23

*Those who do not know how to
weep with their whole hearts
don't know how to laugh, either.*

Golda Meir

We really have little control over our feelings. We can control what we do about them but not the feelings themselves. Addiction causes many losses, many heartaches. Sometimes, just when we think we've accepted the losses and have finished grieving over them, the pain reappears.

We never used to deal with pain. Now we are faced with really feeling and that is scary. It is also good. Eventually, we'll get used to having feelings again. Crying when we're sad is a way of releasing some of the sadness and cleansing our wounds. Crying means we are alive and feeling things again. And as we learn to feel sorrow, we learn to laugh again, too. We learn to feel joy and hope and wonder.

Today let me rejoice in feeling my feelings.

*Why did the children put beans
in their ears when the one thing
we told the children never to do
was put beans in their ears?*

Carl Sandburg

One of the most important jobs of growing up is developing independence. Sometimes, others don't see it that way. We wish they could understand that we need to find our own course in life, and form our own values.

In order to gain independence we need to let our loved ones know how we feel. Making sure they know we are not rejecting them by having our own ideas is a start. We can accomplish this by talking to them about how we feel. Only through understanding can others know and appreciate our struggles toward independence. Maybe they can come to love our differences. And maybe we can come to love and understand them better, too.

Today let me take a step toward independence.

*People asking questions, lost in
confusion. Well, I tell them there's
no problem—only solutions.*

John Lennon

When Alice first discovered the Cheshire
Cat, she asked him, "Would you please tell me
which way I ought to go from here?" "That
depends a great deal on where you want to get
to," answered the cat.

Today we can plan our lives and aim them
in a good orderly direction. When we were
using, there was only confusion and few solutions. Recovery has taught us to live in the
solution and not the problem.

We have 24 hours to plan at a time. Our
future and past lives are not real today. Each
day is a new beginning and by planning and
setting goals, we can make it the kind of day
we want it to be.

*Today let my goal be to look for solutions, not
problems.*

*See what you are becoming. Do
you like the trend of your life? If
not, change it.*

Yogananda

Taking a daily inventory can help us be
the best we can be. A daily inventory of
ourselves keeps us on track and moving in a
positive direction. If we end each day by
writing a list of how our day was—how we
were—we get a good idea of our strengths and
weaknesses. We can look at the strengths as
things we have, and the weaknesses as things
we need to fix. We can walk through each day
more clear-headed by doing this, and we will
find how quickly our lives improve. And that
is what we are all after—improvement.

Today let me begin taking a daily inventory.

*Knowing when to say no and
when to say yes is the beginning
of true wisdom.*

Ralph T. Rupert

Today we know that we are separate people who have our own unique boundaries. We are learning to define ourselves in relationships with others and to clearly tell others what we need.

We are learning that to stay healthy we must set limits. We must have the courage to get honest and say, "No, I won't." At first, we feel guilty when we start taking care of ourselves. But soon we come to enjoy feeling strong. We like asking for our own rights. We begin to enjoy the freedom that comes with knowing we are taking care of ourselves.

Our first job is to learn to take good care of ourselves. Only when healthy and serene, can we be of true service and value to others.

Today let me learn that setting limits is not selfish.

*So live that you wouldn't be
ashamed to sell the family parrot
to the town gossip.*

Will Rogers

Respecting ourselves and others means paying attention to how we talk. It's easy to get into a habit of littering our speech with cruel jokes and curse words. If we find others taking offense at our speech, we can become defensive or we can take a serious look at their comments. It is a humbling experience to admit that we are offending others.

Having decided to clean up our lives, we can also begin to work at finding ways of talking without being offensive. Speech is a powerful tool that allows others to know our deep feelings, opinions, and needs. We deserve to have healthy power in every area of our life, and language is power.

Today let me review how I use language to determine if it is an asset or liability.

*Lighthouses do not ring bells and
fire cannons to call attention to
their shining—they just shine.*

Dwight L. Moody

If someone kindly points out something
about our behavior that is unhealthy and we
react by trying to hurt or frighten them, we
are acting out of false pride. Our pride was
hurt. We felt backed into a corner so we
attacked. If on the other hand, we accepted
the person's observation and made an honest
effort to see if they had a point, we are practicing true pride. True pride helps us feel
safe, because we know we can take care of
ourselves. And we can now honestly listen to
others. With true pride we can love ourselves
enough to grow and learn and be confident
enough to admit we're not perfect.

*Today I will not let false pride prevent me from
growing, asking questions, learning, and
developing.*

*Were the diver to think on the
jaws of the shark he would never
lay hands on the precious pearl.*

Sa'Di

A good way to overcome a fear is to do
what you are afraid of. We often feel we're
different and what works for some people
surely won't work for us. But, of course, this
is just a bad attitude and, like all attitudes, it
can be fixed. So, if we feel too shy to approach
a girl and ask her out, we can call her on the
phone instead.

The important thing is the effort that is
made, not the outcome. The thing to rejoice
about is making the phone call, not whether
or not the girl said yes or no. It's the trying
that will begin to make a change. When we
face our fears, we learn a new self-respect and
courage. Even if things don't go our way,
we're rewarded with a new sense of pride.

Today let me do one thing I find fearful.

August 31

*Morning glories are beautiful
because they open up again and
again.*

Louise Hope

Old habits may become like playing a record with a deep scratch. The more we play the record, the deeper and more annoying the scratch becomes until we finally have to throw the record out.

We are challenged to try new ideas as we let go of the old. We can take daily adventure trips if we are willing to live with an attitude of openness. Being open to different music, new people, and different foods are all experiences in taking a step into the unknown.

The more we can be open to newness, the more we seem to grow in flexibility, and tolerance. What a joy to risk each day and not be locked into rigidity and conformity.

Today let me be open to the experience of exploring new ideas.

*Fate chooses our relatives, we
choose our friends.*

Jacques Delille

Friends are important to us. Sometimes when we feel misunderstood by our parents, we go to our friends. They help when we are hurting. If we are lucky, we have some true friends who really love us.

Some of us have been hurt by people we thought were friends. Some of us have hurt people who thought of us as friends. We must work at friendship. We can't expect our friends to be perfect. True friendship means sharing.

Today we know that to nourish a friendship, we must be honest and talk about our feelings and problems. We are finding that we can't lose with honesty. We are also finding that friendship grows stronger when we face problems together.

Today let me help my friendships grow.

September 2

Consider the postage stamp. It secures success by sticking to one thing until it gets there.

Josh Billings

Dreams can become reality. Every dream starts with a tiny flicker of an idea. Ideas will come to us at the right and perfect time. We can choose to have a fertile, hopeful mind or a stagnant, negative mind. In recovery, we are learning to nurture and be kind to our dreams. We used to be quick to judge ourselves critically. When we had ideas about what we might do or become, negative thinking would squash our ideas before they could grow.

Today we see a new vision of hope in recovery. We can accomplish our goals by the simple art of learning to follow through a day at a time. We are learning to appreciate the fine art of perseverance.

Today let me believe my dreams and follow through.

*True love is not a feeling by which
we're overwhelmed; it is a committed thoughtful decision.*

M. Scott Peck

Passion-filled love can knock us off our
feet. For many of us, the thrill of being overwhelmed was terribly attractive. We loved
living in the storm of passion. Most of us,
though, found we couldn't tolerate this feeling for very long. It is exhausting and confusing. Often, it is frightening. Some of us have
been terribly hurt in these romances.

Now we know that passions raging out of
control are harmful. True love is a healing
force, not a hurting one. When we find true
love, we're nurtured and supported. When we
give true love to another, we find joy and
serenity.

Today let me see my relationships honestly.

September 4

> *He who asks a question is a fool*
> *for five minutes, he who does not*
> *ask a question remains a fool*
> *forever.*

> *Chinese Proverb*

A large ego is the enemy of learning. The first step in learning and growing is to admit we don't have all the answers.

We're learning to respect our need to know. We are learning the value of taking risks and asking for what we need. Sitting in silence is a lonely experience. Sometimes, our seemingly dumb question is one everyone else was afraid to ask. By taking an active part in our own education, we find we are not isolated. In this way, we take an active role in our own growth.

Today let me have the courage to ask what I want to know.

*Healthy rituals are the padding
that round out the rough edges of
life.*

Joann Burnes

Rituals can be healthy when they give our lives order and direction. Having goals and setting up a schedule put us in the right frame of mind to meet the new day.

A morning prayer or quiet time will help us stay focused and accomplish the tasks for that day. Entering our day at a whirlwind pace usually produces anxiety and confusion. What a difference a few minutes in the morning can make in our overall serenity.

Whatever makes us feel better and is refreshing is worth developing in our lives. When we give ourselves a healthy structure to grow with, we add to the strength we are feeling inside, and we bring new balance and purpose to each day.

Today let me start to establish healthy rituals.

September 6

*Disputes are inevitable. The first
step toward winning: control
yourself.*

Arch Lustberg

Our anger takes the driver's seat when
our egos are in charge. Only a big ego demands that we be right by angrily attacking
another human being. Proving that we are
right by putting someone else down is a sure
way to lose our serenity.

We are in control of our tempers today.
We know now that we don't have to give up
control. We can listen and we can disagree
without becoming angry. We can speak calmly
for ourselves today. No longer at the mercy of
our ego or our temper, we feel a new strength
and confidence in ourselves.

*Today let me remember that I have a choice
about how to express my anger.*

*Every great mistake has a half-
way moment, a split second when
it can be recalled and perhaps
remedied.*

Pearl S. Buck

All of us can recall a time when we knew
we were about to do or say something against
our better judgment. Once we might not have
been able to stop. We were slaves to our
runaway thoughts and behaviors. Being in
control of our own behavior is a new and
wonderful feeling. As we master ourselves
more each day, we find a great sense of serenity, a new peace. Now we are free. Free to
think for ourselves and free to do the next
right thing because we want to.

*Today let me remember that it's never too late
to change.*

September 8

*Oh God: I am grateful to You for
having given me this life.*

Etty Hillesum

For many of us, life didn't seem to be
something to be grateful for. We may have
had sad, disrupted childhoods. We often felt
like no one cared whether we were alive or
not. We couldn't imagine our lives ever getting better.

Now we can. We are recovering and our
lives are taking on a whole new shape. We get
glimmers of happiness and they are starting
to wipe away the darkness that used to engulf
our lives. Those glimmers of happiness can
grow into hours and days of joy and peace. We
begin to trust that years of happiness lie
ahead, if we stay on the path of recovery.
Today we can be truly grateful for our lives.
We can honestly thank our Higher Power for
the gift of life.

Today let me remember to be grateful.

We have the power to direct our minds to replace the feelings of being upset, depressed, and fearful with the feeling of inner peace.

Gerald G. Jampolsky

Learning to identify negative thoughts is a powerful way to begin changing our negative behavior. We always think before we act, even if the thinking has become automatic. We have the power to change our thinking.

As we become committed to being aware of negative thoughts, we can stop, take a deep breath, and repeat a positive affirmation. Practicing this process will actually change the way we feel about ourselves. By thinking about positive things, we can change how we feel about the situation and about ourselves, too. Now, life has more promise, more joy.

Today let me have the courage to change the way I think.

September 10

*The greatest thing in the world is
to know how to belong to oneself.*

Montaigne

There is nothing wrong in loving and
caring for others but it becomes a problem
when we neglect our own needs. We need to
put ourselves on our please list even if it
means taking some of the time we used to
please others. It is impossible to care for
ourselves when we are focused on others. But
we can learn to change by treating ourselves
as well as we do other people. We can respect
our own needs and wishes, give ourselves a
break, some extra attention, even a gift. We
can learn to love others as we love ourselves,
not better than we love ourselves.

*Today let me realize that only by caring for
myself first will I have the energy and love to
give to others.*

*It amazes me that when I ask for
sobriety each day, I actually get
it—and more!*

Ruth C.

When we remember to ask God to help us
each morning, and thank Him for our recovery before we fall asleep at night, we also
thank ourselves. This simple method puts
bookends on our days. Our Twelve Step program, our friends and loved ones, and our
Higher Power help us to recover. But we do
the job ourselves. In thanking God, we're
thanking Him for the strength to get through
the day sober and clean. We're thanking Him
for helping us succeed.

Repeated prayer and sincere willingness
to stay sober work. Prayer is the natural
remedy of our program.

Today let me pray as if my life depended on it!

September 12

The first wealth is health.

Ralph Waldo Emerson

If we found a tiny baby bird with a broken wing, we wouldn't just toss it in the air and say "You're young—fly!" Of course not. We would probably hold it gently and feed it with a medicine dropper and slowly nurture it back to health. And then, when it is completely healed, we let it go. It's this kind of tenderness that we need for ourselves as we start to heal from a serious disease.

Wellness is not just having one part of us well, it's having all our parts well. We need to combine exercise, good nutrition, rest, and emotional health to achieve a balanced sense of well-being. Our emotional strength will come from working at our recovery, praying, and meditating.

Today let me treat myself with gentle, healing acts.

Find a point of love.

Charles Fillmore

Charles Fillmore was the founder of the Unity Church. He said that in every person and situation there is some point to love and our challenge is to find it.

Some days others make us mad and we find one fault after another in them. One thing leads to another and our thinking becomes sick. We may wonder if there is any point to even trying to love people. Keeping a relationship going often seems like very hard work. It's worth it, though.

Now, we take better care of ourselves, instead of expecting others to take care of us. We handle our anger and resentment. We have found ways to deal with conflict and are strong enough to take care of ourselves. We can see how important relationships are to us.

Today let me work through the problems in my relationships.

*If at first you don't succeed, you're
running about average.*

M. H. Alderson

No one has it all. No one succeeds at
everything. Some people do well in sports,
some are musically talented, some are good at
organizing. If we could hold out both hands
and place our weaknesses in one hand and
our strengths in the other, we would probably
have evenly distributed handfuls.

The problem is most of us usually hold the
handful of weaknesses behind our backs, so
all others can see is the hand with the
strengths. And we think mostly about the
handful of weaknesses behind our backs. In
recovery, we learn to accept both sides. Now,
we don't have to hide our weaknesses from
others. And we can love our strengths. Now,
we've found the real strength of recovery.

*Today let me see both my weaknesses and my
strengths realistically.*

*Our deeds determine us as much
as we determine our deeds.*

George Eliot

Today we understand the importance of planning. We are dealing with our lives. It can be dangerous to just let them happen. Setting priorities is like making a budget: a budget for time, money, sleep, homework, and so on. If we plan our budgets in advance, we'll be prepared to act on plan instead of impulse.

In recovery, we are not at the mercy of our impulses. We feel safer, knowing our lives are in control. We know how to provide what we need, and we know when we need it. A plan can help us control our time even better, and avoid the impulses that can lead to relapse.

Today let me start to set priorities and make plans.

September 16

*Acting without thinking can lead
to drinking.*

Joe Williams

Rebellion can become a sickness of the spirit and devour us. Part of the task of growing is to separate from our parents. Only by making our own life decisions can we become independent. Sometimes our struggle for independence gets fueled by rage and we rebel. We're like runaway trains that smash everything in our way.

By learning to think ahead, we can see where an action might lead us, and we can see the consequences we might have to pay. We can ask ourselves if a moment of rebellion is worth risking our life-long recovery. We can look ahead and make choices based on our long-term needs, not the impulse of the moment. Now, we can make healthy choices.

Today let me have the patience to stop, wait, and think before I act.

*Love your enemy, it will drive
him nuts.*

Eleanor Doan

When we are able to be nice and gracious
to someone we don't like we are given great
personal power. We are finding that the only
real power in our world comes from deep
inside us. Having inner ease and the sure
knowledge that no one can take away our
serenity gives us confidence and self-esteem
beyond measure.

Praying for our enemy will help us step
back and be more objective about our anger.
Is it worth giving up our serenity? By making
a positive response instead of a negative one,
by praying or loving instead of resenting, we
turn an enemy into an opportunity for our
own growth. When an enemy becomes an
asset like this, it's easy to love him.

*Today let me pray for my enemy and see if my
burden isn't lifted.*

September 18

When people talk, listen com-
pletely. Most people never listen.

Ernest Hemingway

Good listeners have lots of friends because they make others feel special and important. Finding a balance between talking
and listening will open new doors in our
relationships with others. What joy we find in
really hearing someone else's story without
waiting to find a pause in the conversation to
jump in and interrupt.

Good friendships seem to be more like the
ebb and flow of the tides. Back and forth,
talking and listening, giving and taking.

Developing the loving art of listening well
to others will bring to us the best in our family
and friends while giving us a way to grow and
learn in our relationships.

Today let me be reminded that it is difficult to
learn if my mouth is always in gear.

*Health nuts are going to feel
stupid some day lying in
hospitals dying of nothing.*

Redd Foxx

As addicts we tend to have a black-and-white way of looking at things. If we can't be the queen of aerobics or the king of weight lifting, we don't want to do anything. But if we allow ourselves to find some middle ground, we'll get where we're going. Most of us know from experience that whenever we do something all-out, we usually burn out.

Runners know that the first one off the line is not always the winner. The race almost always goes to the one who is consistent with a steady stride. We can start our race by choosing one small thing to get some exercise. Even something as small as parking at the end of the lot and walking is a good start.

Today let me allow my recovering body some small exercise.

September 20

*Politeness goes far, yet costs
nothing.*

Samuel Smites

When other kids were practicing how to
act during job interviews, we may have been
doing drugs. When others were working or
playing sports, were we high? When others
were learning about relationships with the
opposite sex, were we drunk? When others
were doing things with their families and
observing adult behavior, where were we?

Where were we? We were gone. But now
we're back and we can learn. It's never too
late to learn. Each sober day, we learn more
and more about how to live. We can learn and
we can teach others what we've learned. We
really do have whole new lives in front of us.

Today let me learn from watching others.

*Just because you feel guilty
doesn't make it true.*

       Lynn B. Daugherty

Many of us are tortured by the guilt of something we did in the past. There often is a deep spiritual pain that seems to fester in our hearts. We can't seem to accept the idea that what is done is done and now we're working hard to be good, honest human beings. It's hard to believe that there is no need for guilt. We are no longer guilty. That's past.

We can free ourselves of the guilt if we look at the pain as a doorway. The only way out of it is to face it and walk through. This is what our fellowship is for. We pray for the courage to share with someone we trust, then we talk. When we do, we're relieved to see that others still accept us. We've discovered that we're not alone and that we are good people.

Today help me be courageous in reviewing my life.

September 22

Change is the law of life.

John F. Kennedy

Little steps and small changes are what big changes are made of. Learning to be good to ourselves is a process that begins with a willing attitude and one small change.

We usually get discouraged and sabotage our progress when we try to do a quick fix on our lives. If we don't like reading, we might begin with one page a day. Perhaps our diets are full of junk foods and lacking fruits and vegetables. We can add health to our meals by drinking a glass of orange juice each morning. Having fourteen people we intensely dislike, we begin by being able to forgive one of the fourteen. We cannot change our lives overnight, but we can change.

A willingness to do one small thing each day will add up to big changes in time.

Today let me be willing to take one area of my life and change one thing about it.

Sleep is the best cure for waking troubles.

Miguel Cervantes

Lack of sleep, or sleep deprivation, is a very serious condition. That old saying, "I'm so tired I can't think straight," is true. If we don't get enough sleep, we can't think clearly and our judgment is impaired. Our reaction time is slow and little problems seem like monster problems.

Our bodies are like batteries. We have enough "juice" to last for about sixteen hours and if we don't recharge ourselves by resting, our ability to operate diminishes.

A good night's sleep is the most powerful energizer of all. We wake refreshed, cheerful, and optimistic. Yesterday's troubles may still be with us, but today they are pint-sized when yesterday they seemed gigantic.

Today give me the strength to value my recovering body enough to give it rest.

He who laughs, lasts.

Mary Pettibone Poole

One of the best feelings in the world is to laugh so hard that tears come to our eyes. There is joy all around us. Sure, there are serious things that must be addressed, but we can always choose to see the joy.

There is joy in music, in nature, in jokes, in watching people, in work. Life is meant to be fun, to be an adventure, to be enjoyed. There is joy almost everywhere we look, if only we look. Every day brings the chance for a smile or giggle, a little nugget of happiness, a fresh gift of life. Joy and laughter are all around us, waiting to be shared.

Today let me see the joy in life.

*To love oneself is the beginning of
a life-long romance.*

Oscar Wilde

For every negative thing about us, we
have a hundred wonderful things. Poor self-
esteem can mask our gifts and rob us of the
ability to accept our own goodness. No matter
what we've done, we can still be good people.

Negativity and self-blame are poisonous.
They silently eat us up inside until we feel like
a piece of Swiss cheese.

It is possible to begin to heal our damaged
self-esteem and start to love ourselves by
deciding to make some positive changes . We
don't need to know the solution at first, all we
need is the willingness to get help. To begin
to heal, we will need to risk and ask one
trustworthy person for help. Honestly talking about our low self-esteem will begin the
healing process.

Today let me be willing to ask for help.

September 26

*Growth is the only evidence of
life.*

Cardinal G. H. Newman

Our personal growth sometimes seems to
happen behind our backs. Since there are no
thunderbolts and headlines, no cheering
crowds, ribbons to cut, or speeches to make,
we don't always recognize how much we've
grown.

But we are changing all the time, every
day. Each healthy choice we make brings us
more self-respect and confidence. Every right
thing we do brings more security and self-
assurance. The choices may be small, but just
as the grass grows without our noticing it, we
are growing each day, too.

*Today let me remember that I am a winner
because I am growing.*

*Keep a watchful eye, for a miracle
you may find. For if your eyes are
closed, it may pass under your
nose.*

Tim Tobin

Nothing happens by mistake and there
are no coincidences in our world. If we believe
that our Higher Power is in charge of our
lives, we might begin to look for His daily
miracles. How many times have we heard the
words we needed or met a special person at
the exact right time? When everything seems
at its darkest, we usually get help at the
perfect moment.

Keeping our eyes and ears open to the
little acts of love in our lives can create a
miracle consciousness. We start to look at the
world from expectant eyes. When we jog with
God as our running mate, we begin to fully
appreciate the scenery along the way.

Today let me expect a miracle.

September 28

Hope is the word which God has written on the brow of every man.

Victor Hugo

Hope's flame lies deep in our hearts and never loses its power to ignite when called upon. We find it hard to understand and explain hope—it just is. It is there for us in the most gut-wrenching and difficult times, waiting for us to reach out our hand. We may have to suffer confusion, but on the other side of our misery we will find a bigger joy waiting.

Perhaps hope is the way God takes care of us in our fears. It is His way of giving us the gift of His grace. Hope is no fair weather friend that runs away and deserts us. It's a true friend that is along for the whole ride, a friend that stays with us through the good and difficult days of our lives. Hope will always be there if we raise our eyes and trust for a second.

Today let me feel the power of hope in my life.

Decisions are like Jello molds.
They only turn out firm when the
right amount of water is added.

Roy Palm

A big decision is like a mountain built on a million small rocks. When we find ourselves stuck and feeling paralyzed about making a big decision, perhaps it is because we didn't pay attention to how we stacked the little rocks.

We may develop the habit of being less than honest in our little decisions. Neglecting and avoiding our needs in small decisions may cause us to feel confused when we need to make big choices. Facing small choices honestly gives us a solid base and allows us to freely face the mountains in our lives. When we look at it this way, it's easy to see how important today's small decisions are.

Today let me make all of my decisions—big and small—honestly and courageously.

*Being in great physical shape is
like having a two-way ticket to
everywhere.*

Mary Hines

Our bodies can be used in hundreds of healthy, creative ways. Our personal challenge is to discover what form of play and recreation suits us best. What do we do that makes us feel that it's great to be alive? What activity brings us surging joy and vitality?

Our bodies need regular recreation breaks, special times to stretch, run, swim, dance, or work out. Taking the time to set up a regular recreation and exercise schedule will help make physical activity a part of our daily routine. We can build a lifetime habit in just three months. Regular weekly activity will soon add up to three months and we will love the way we look and feel.

Today let me make a commitment to take good care of myself physically.

*Grudges and resentments are like
strings of rocks tied around our
necks. Every time we add a rock,
we increase our pain load.*

Ralph Sobostra

Resentment robs us of peace. Resentments don't hurt other people, they hurt us.
As we become obsessed with our anger, the
people who make us mad usually go merrily
on their way, unaware of our feelings.

Forgiveness is the shovel that will dig us
out of the hole of pain caused by our grudges.
We sometimes feel like we are giving up when
we forgive someone. We don't feel they deserve anything, much less to be forgiven.
Forgiveness is a gift we give to ourselves.

Forgiveness doesn't mean that we accept
unacceptable behavior. It just means we are
living in today by burying our old pain.

*Today let me know that forgiveness is a gift
that I give myself.*

October 2

*Resolve to be thyself; and know,
that he who finds himself, loses
his misery.*

Matthew Arnold

We all have known the braggarts, the boastful ones who constantly toot their own horns. These people crave approval because they don't yet approve of themselves. There are those who do the same thing but they're not so noisy about it. The girl who says she's ugly even though she's pretty, or the guy who says he's dumb even though he isn't. These are not humble people. They are people who need to learn to approve of themselves.

We don't have to be either of these people now. We can honestly look at ourselves and see our strengths and weaknesses for what they are. We don't have to put ourselves down today. Best of all, we can now accept compliments graciously.

Today I will make an effort to accept myself.

*I wish my parents would trust me
and understand that I am trying
my hardest.*

Anonymous

Our parents are hard to understand at
times. Sometimes they give double messages.
They tell us what is really important is that
we try our hardest. Then they seem crushed
when we do try our hardest but don't do as
well as they expected. We sometimes wish
they would stop getting themselves mixed up
in us. We don't always want the things they
want for us.

We hope our parents know that we're
really trying. It's true that we'll make mistakes, but isn't that normal? It might help if
we knew more about what it was like for them
growing up. Maybe it's time to risk asking
them.

*Today let me get to know my parents a little
better.*

October 4

Birds sing after a storm. Why shouldn't we?

Rose Kennedy

Some of us have been through an awful lot. We have endured pain and hopelessness. Now we have some choices to make. We can allow our pasts to make us feel badly about ourselves or we can sing after the storm. We can feel proud that we are not giving up, we are not willing to be destroyed.

The past won't change, and the bad things won't magically go away. But we can learn to move forward.

We can put the past where it belongs, close enough so we'll never forget, and far enough away so we don't give it all of our attention. The sun doesn't just make rainbows for other people, they're for us too.

Today let me tell myself that it's okay to feel good about myself.

*Anything in anyway beautful
derives its beauty from itself.*

Marcus Aurelius

Why are we critical of ourselves? We can accept imperfections in our friends a lot easier than we accept them in ourselves. We are our own worst critics.

In our recovery, we are learning to have pride in our accomplishments. We can see the little improvements in our lives and know we are responsible for them.

Little by little we are beginning to realize that it is important for us to accept ourselves as we really are. We are each beautiful in our own unique ways. We are children of God and have everything we need for today.

Today let me select one good thing about myself and remember it . . . no matter what.

October 6

Silence gives consent.

Oliver Goldsmith

With active addiction there is usually little effective communication. We learned to shout and threaten, rather than listen and speak for ourselves.

We must work at improving communication, or we'll fall back into the old patterns. Learning to communicate is not easy, but it's also not impossible. Often we just need to learn to listen. If we don't know what the other person is trying to say, we can't possibly understand. When we really listen, we learn all kinds of new things, sometimes important things. And in listening to others, we set a good example for them to follow when listening to us. In listening to others, we learn how to say what we feel.

Today let me make an effort to communicate.

*There is nothing greater in life
than loving another and being
loved in return, for loving is the
ultimate of experiences.*

Leo F. Buscaglia

In true love there is no room for game-playing. There is no room for trying to attract someone and then dropping them when we've won. There is no room for taking advantage of those we can manipulate and control. In true love, there is no room for lies, cruel sarcasm, or hiding our true selves.

In true love there is comfort—pure, relaxing comfort. Oh yes, the excitement, the butterflies-in-the-stomach are present, but still there is a peaceful comfort when two people know each other's hearts, love what they've found, and feel perfectly free to say exactly what their feelings are.

Today I will try to act more loving in all my relationships.

October 8

*Courage: The power to let go of
the familiar.*

Raymond Lindquist

Some days our recovery demands giant doses of courage. It is so hard to let go of slippery people, places, and things. We still miss our old using friends. Knowing that they're not good for us doesn't take the missing away. We feel like we're stuck in the middle between yesterday and tomorrow. We are. It's a place called today.

Living in the present is a courageous act. Our old familiar life is full of pain and regrets, but it is familiar. Deep inside, though, we know that being clean and sober is the best hope we have for ourselves. Today we can be brave and face what each day brings with courage and the knowledge that we are doing the right thing for ourselves.

Today let me have the courage to believe that the best is yet to come.

*This is the day which the Lord
has made; we will rejoice and be
glad in it.*

Psalms 118:24

We are grateful to be alive today. Sobriety is teaching us about ways to have natural fun. We are even beginning to enjoy our own company. There are little joys to see every day. Now we are capable of seeing them.

Our joy begins when we allow space for it. We can do this by just living in the moment and enjoying life as it is happening—not getting distracted by yesterday's angers or fears of tomorrow.

When we wake up to a sunny day, we can smile and get ourselves out in the beautiful weather. If we wake up to a rainy day, we can appreciate the need for such days and still be happy. We know now that we are as happy as we decide to be.

Today let me be grateful for this day.

*I really have become stronger at
the broken places.*

Max Cleland

Captain Max Cleland lost both his legs
and his left arm in Vietnam. He turned his
disability into many opportunities including
his election as a U.S. senator and Georgia's
Secretary of State. He became a good day
expert and a genius in victorious living. Max
Cleland believes that to be truly successful we
must strive for acceptance of our problems,
concentrate on the doors in our lives that are
opening instead of the ones that have been
closed, and let God help us.

We, too, have broken places that can
become our strongest places. We know now
that we can learn from our hurts and disap-
pointments and become better people because
of them. With the help of God, we are becoming stronger than we ever dreamed possible.

Today let me look for the open doors in my life.

Not he who has much is rich, but
he who gives much.

Erich Fromm

The idea of service is new to us. We never had time to focus on the needs of others when we were using. Others were only there to be used for our benefit. If they couldn't be used, they were just in the way.

Now we are learning to bend our stubborn self-centered wills. We are learning to be of real help to others. Sometimes we find that our biggest service is to keep quiet and listen. It's not possible for us to really listen to others when we are thinking about our reply. We are beginning to believe that we don't need to have all of the answers for someone else. We can share our own experiences when the time is right.

Today let me be of service to others.

October 12

*You are only the channel through
which divine action takes place...*

Emmet Fox

We all need a way of finding peace and
relief from any worry or problem. We can do
this by praying about our problem or worry
for a short while. Then we simply let go and
turn the problem completely over to the care
of our Higher Power, making a decision not to
think or worry about it anymore.

We can control our own thinking. It's a
matter of simply choosing which thoughts we
pay attention to. To use our choice in this way
is to exercise our own power in our lives.
When we find the problem in our consciousness, we can switch our thoughts to our Higher
Power. If we concentrate on His love and
peace and say a short comforting prayer, we
won't take the problem back.

*Today let me learn to turn my problems over to
my Higher Power.*

*I give away my personal power
when I put on boxing gloves and
enter the ring with authority.*

Clayton Smith

The more we resist authority, the more we resist recovery. Learning to accept authority in life is essential for our happiness.

When we resist, it might help to question our feelings. Do we get angry when we are told what to do? What do we feel we need to prove by resisting authority? What deeper emotions might be hidden under our anger? Why do we keep having to prove our power and worth?

The more we are able to inventory and explore our resistance, the less power it will have over us. The fact of life is that the more we learn to say yes, the more we'll feel truly powerful.

Today let me swallow my ego and learn how to deal with authority.

October 14

*Exercise relieves stress, gets you
in shape and most of all makes
you feel good about yourself.*

Murphy Tobin

Exercise is a natural health tonic. It squeezes out our stress and tensions and gives our bodies a way to be rejuvenated. At times we resist the discipline and structure exercise asks of us. We talk ourselves into putting off our program until tomorrow, saying that we really will begin on Monday. Mondays have a way of becoming next Mondays when we put off caring for our bodies.

We get great feelings of well-being, pride, and accomplishment from exercise. We wonder what took us so long to get started when the results are so uplifting and outstanding. After a while, we find that exercise becomes like breathing—a natural part of our lives.

Today let me enjoy my exercise and feel gratitude for my ability to take care of myself.

*Three decays surround the
modern young: The decay of care
and skill, the decay of enterprise
and adventure, the decay of
compassion.*

Kurt Hahn

Recovery can be a call to skill building, adventure, and compassion. Our true spirit couldn't emerge when we were numb from using. Today we are on a great adventure. We can go as far as our dreams will allow.

We are involved in our own personal life adventures and we have options today. There is so much excitement in expanding our horizons and making our dreams a reality.

All we need for this is the willingness to ask for and accept help, and the willingness to take one step at a time. By living in the present we live life to its fullest, and that's the most we can ask of ourselves.

Today let me appreciate the adventure.

October 16

Each day the world is born anew
For him who take it rightly.

James Russell Lowell

Today may be just another day for many people, but for us in recovery it is a fresh, new, never-been-used day. It is a new page on which we can write the story of our choice.

If we have sobriety, that is the finest gift we'll ever receive because it prepares us to receive all other gifts life can bring. Without sobriety, we can't handle gifts like love, self-esteem, serenity, fun, and relationships. So even if we don't have everything we'd like to have today, like more money or better family relationships, we have the grandest gift of all, sobriety and fellowship.

We are success stories, and even if they don't come all wrapped up with ribbons and bows, our lives can be opened each day and admired anew.

Today let me live my life as if it's brand new.

*Do not consider painful what is
good for you.*

Euripides

"Clean your room, take a shower, wash
that dirty shirt." What a drag it is to be
nagged at about how we look or smell. We
may purposely not wash or clean our rooms to
prove we have the right to run our own lives.

Rebellion may be great for a while, but
sooner or later we will get tired of the clutter,
dirt, and smell. How do we start being cleaner
without feeling we are selling out?

Taking good care of our hygiene and
appearance is something we do for us even if
it also pleases others. By deciding we enjoy
some order and cleanliness in our lives, we
choose to develop it. When we see how we feel
about being clean, we will wonder why we
didn't do such nice things for ourselves sooner.

*Today let me start to change habits that are
hurting me.*

October 18

Over my slumber your loving
watch keep. Rock me to sleep,
mother; rock me to sleep.

When we use drugs, the body's ability to regulate itself is impaired. Before drugs, our bodies were able to tell us, "You're tired," or "You're ill." After using chemicals, our bodies may be in desperate need, but the message never gets to our brains, or it gets garbled.

Our bodies are beginning to learn to function normally again. Our systems are trying to give us the proper messages, but it takes time to get everything back in working order. Until then, we can apply common sense. We may not feel tired, but common sense tells us that if we don't get enough sleep tonight, we'll be dragging tomorrow. If we see the results of using our common sense, soon we will learn to trust our bodies again.

Today let me take care of my body sensibly.

*Being interested in others will
create more friendships for you
than trying to make others
interested in you.*

Judy Zerefa

The best way to have a friend is to be one. We learned the hard way when it came to friendships. We were never able to keep friends for long. The only thing we shared were drugs and alcohol. Many of us felt sad with our friends. No one really listened.

In recovery we are learning how to listen to others. We know now that we can't learn anything with our mouths open. When we begin to really hear our friends, an amazing thing starts to happen. We begin to feel happier. What a relief! Being interested in others is a gift we can cherish. It is also a gift that gives back to us, because it enriches our friendships.

Today let me learn to care.

October 20

*Trusting takes courage. The best
way to start trusting is simply to
start trusting.*

John Wilson

Trust is a two way street. How do others
treat me and how do I respond to others?
These are important questions to ask.

Sometimes we long for trust and closeness but are afraid to let people know of our
needs. We are afraid we might be hurt if we
expose our feelings. So we build walls of
anger and isolation. We feel hurt and angry
because our needs aren't being met.

It may have been a long time since we
trusted anyone. We know now that we must
trust. Trusting and being trusted gives us a
freedom we've never known before. We no
longer have to go it alone when we trust
others. This lets the light of new power into
our lives.

Today let me learn to trust.

*Building love is like building a
house. It takes a lot of hard work
and sweat before we have a safe,
cozy place to share.*

S. M. McHugh

There is a famous rock star who never
wrote any love songs. He said he didn't want
to contribute to the fantasy that love was the
cure-all of life's problems. Songs, movies,
fairy tales, and TV brainwash young people
into believing that love will fix everything.

Do we know that love relationships are
often hard work? Do we know that our happiness depends on us and that without really
loving ourselves we can't love anyone else?

These are hard lessons to learn. Sometimes we learn by enjoying the rewards of
self-love and independence. When we begin
to feel these things, we attract other healthy
people into our lives.

Today let me better understand real love.

October 22

I never notice what has been done. I only see what remains to be done.

Madam Curie

We should praise ourselves for each thing we do to make ourselves healthy and sober, but the praise should be, "I'm doing well, I'm getting healthy and sober," rather than, "I did a great job, thank God that's over." We never finish the job of becoming healthy, whole people.

No matter how much we've done, there are always new jobs, new challenges to be met. Today we can measure our progress in security, peace of mind, and the earned love of others. But the more healthy we become, the more joy is waiting for us. We don't ever have to settle for less again.

Today let me do my best for just one day.

A man cannot be comfortable
without his own approval.

Mark Twain

Deep down, we all want our parents or family to approve of us. But some people can't give us approval because they never got their approval when they were young. When we realize this, we can begin to let go.

This is sad, but when we let go of them, we're also letting go of an old part of ourselves. Inside we always believed there was something wrong with us. What other reason would they have for being so critical?

It will be hard at first to love and accept ourselves because we have gotten used to feeling bad. But when we come to believe we are really good people, it will change our thinking about a lot of things in life. It will open us up to others, release energy for growth, and give us serenity at last.

Today help me accept my goodness.

October 24

. . . I was quite certain that no matter where I was in the world I would always find stars and be able to flop down on a bed or a floor, or anywhere else, and feel absolutely at home.

Etty Hillesum

We carry our serenity in our hearts and it can remain with us no matter where our life journeys take us. The only time we feel absolutely at home is when we are at peace with ourselves. There is a certain rightness and sense of security that serenity brings us. Nothing can disturb that peace.

Once we've found that kind of peace, we are willing to go to any length to keep it. We sometimes need to stand guard over our serenity. No person, place, or thing is worth giving up our peace of mind for.

Today let me remember that peace of mind is a gift to be cherished.

> *Discouragement is a kind of*
> *retreat where we can escape*
> *reality and soothe ourselves in*
> *self-pity.*

> *Norman Vincent Peale*

Self-pity is seductive company. At first, we seem to enjoy feeling sorry for ourselves. It feels good to sink into the depths of the poor me's. Self-pity, though, is a traitor.

Sobriety teaches us that self-pity can't be trusted. When our thinking gets to stinking, we start sinking. We don't have to be seduced by self-pity today. Today we know that nothing is all that bad. We have learned how to face our problems and find answers. We can give up being victims of our own or other people's problems. We can learn to love the light instead of the darkness. We can find joy in self-reliance instead of self-pity.

Today let me remember that there is nothing as pitiful as self-pity.

*Life is not merely living but living
in health.*

Martial

When we brush our teeth we don't brush
just a few, we brush them all because there's
no point in doing the job half-way. That's the
way it is with our whole bodies. What's the
point of exercising and afterwards eating junk
food? Or eating a well-rounded meal but not
bathing? Our bodies are the houses we live in,
the only ones we have.

Many people put more time and concern
into caring for their cars than they do into
caring for the only body they've got. We don't
have to follow that example. We can start
today to make amends to our physical selves.
We can begin to treat our bodies with the
respect they deserve but never got before. We
can eat right, sleep right, and exercise to show
ourselves how truly important we are.

Today I'll treat my body with love.

*Each time a man stands up for
an ideal, or acts to improve the
lot of others, or strikes out
against injustice, he sends forth a
tiny ripple of hope.*

Robert Kennedy

We can make a difference in our world today. To be clean and sober we need to take a personal stand. Our recovery belongs only to us. It is the first thing in our lives that is truly ours. Every time we say no, we stand up for ourselves. All these refusals add up and are teaching us to say yes to life.

Today we choose to be free and experience life as it really is. We can take the rough edges and ride the waves. Today we truly belong to ourselves. We are no longer slaves to our addiction. We have ourselves, our programs, friends, family, and above all, we are protected by our Higher Power.

Today let me embrace all of life.

October 28

Pride goeth before destruction,
and a haughty spirit before a fall.

Proverbs 16:18

If we are not always right, what will people think? If we own up to a mistake and admit we were wrong, will others dance circles around us singing "Ha ha! You were wrong!"

Our egos can be so powerful we'll imagine all sorts of things to keep from admitting we're wrong. We are so sure that others will think less of us if we admit a mistake that we'll go to great lengths to argue the point when it would have been easier and more true to simply say, "I was wrong."

The truth is, people think more highly of us when we demonstrate the maturity of admitting fault. When we do admit we're wrong, it's like adding a medal to our chest. It's a good, firm step forward in recovery.

Today I'll try to admit when I'm wrong.

Get away from the crowd when you can. Keep yourself to yourself, if only for a few hours daily.

Arthur Brisbane

Recovery asks that we make friends with ourselves. Learning to spend some time alone is hard for many of us. We avoided being quiet with ourselves in the past. Some of us feel as if we have an empty hole in our gut.

In recovery, there is no way to avoid confronting the empty feeling. Learning to sit with our anxiety and restlessness is healing. Talking about our new feelings with others is the best remedy for the pain and fear.

By sharing our pain, we fill that emptiness with love, support, and understanding. This comes from others who know and care for us, but most importantly from within us, as we begin to do caring things for ourselves.

Today let me grow to appreciate myself in quiet moments.

October 30

The last link is broken
That bound me to thee,
And the words thou last spoken
Have rendered me free.

Fanny Steers

We've heard the expression, "You are what
you eat," and it could just as easily read, "You
are who you hang out with." If we associate
with sober people who are working at their
recovery, we'll probably be like them. And the
opposite is true too. If we hang out with
people who use, we'll end up using again.

We need to trust that our Higher Power
will show us answers to questions about our
old friends. We must remember that our fellowship of recovering people is a Power greater
than us. Our sponsor and the program will
show us the way if only we ask. Even if we
don't particularly like the answer, we'll be
grateful for the sanity it represents.

Today let me use my recovery resources.

*How can I believe in God when
just last week I got my tongue
caught in the roller of an electric
typewriter?*

Woody Allen

If our introduction to religion and God
was filled with threats of punishment and
hell it would make perfect sense for us not to
want to believe in something so scary. Even
though we may have been taught that God is
love, we may not have witnessed a lot of God's
love in action.

All we are asked to do in recovery is to
believe in a Higher Power. That could mean
God, or it could simply mean the sober people
who are helping us to recover. Our Higher
Power is there, watching over us, ready to be
seen in any way we are willing and able to see.

*Today let me decide for me what kind of God
I believe in.*

November 1

*Love doesn't just sit there like a
stone, it has to be made, like
bread; remade all the time, made
new.*

Ursula K. LeGuin

Love is a gift. Today we have the chance
to love others. We used to believe love meant
letting someone else take care of our needs.
We used to expect people to keep loving us no
matter how we treated them. Somehow we
never understood how to love someone else.

Today we believe love at its best is our
willingness to know others as they are. We
want to love today because it feels good to get
out of our small world and give to someone
else. Love is built on small acts of kindness
and moments of acceptance.

*Today let me cherish the people I meet and
offer them my attention.*

*In your prayer, do not hesitate to
thank the Lord for all that He
gives.*

Chris Aridas

What kind of gift is addiction? Is it a gift
to have flawed parents? These are gifts in a
way because they allow us to start developing
courage, knowledge, and tolerance.

These are things that force us to look deep
inside ourselves where it's scary and yet exciting, to find the strength that lives there. If
we were not forced to look at what's inside of
us, what kind of people might we be? People
who've never struggled and experienced things
improving through hard work and patience
are usually not equipped to handle life's troubles later on. We've seen a bad situation get
better, and we know how to work to improve
it. What better gift could we have?

*Today let me look on my troubles as gifts and
opportunities.*

November 3

*Success can make you go one of
two ways. It can make you a
prima donna, or it can smooth
away the insecurities, let the nice
things come out.*

Barbara Walters

Most of us think of success as things like
becoming a professional athlete or being a
movie star. If that's what we think success is,
no wonder we don't all feel terribly successful.

If we consider a star athlete successful, it
is not because of his current status. It's
because of all the successes he had to create in
his life in order to get where he is. It's the
small, day-to-day achievements that made
him a success. That is what success is for all
of us, a series of events and choices. It's not
the end result that's important, but the series
of choices that make for successful living.

*Today I will be a success and work towards
creating a better life for myself.*

Experience teaches you to recognize a mistake when you've made it again.

Anonymous

If we are human, we will make mistakes. All of us, no matter how carefully we work at our recovery, no matter how hard we try, will make mistakes. There's nothing wrong about making mistakes, and we can choose to comfort ourselves when we've made one instead of shaming ourselves about it. Shaming ourselves will only keep us from getting help.

If we think well of ourselves and believe we have a right to heal and be happy, we'll be more likely to get help.

When we are kind and compassionate to ourselves, we are more likely to stay in recovery. We will also end up reaping the rewards, like knowing, accepting, and loving ourselves.

Today let me love myself no matter what mistakes I make.

I love you just the way you are.

Billy Joel

We accept and love our friends, why can't we accept ourselves? We are often our own worst enemies when it comes to loving ourselves just the way we are. Do we really believe that we are exactly as we should be today with all of our strengths and flaws? Every one of us has qualities we would like to change, but change takes time.

Imagine loving ourselves as much as we can today, with no judgments. How do we treat our best friend? We take the good times along with the bad. Don't we owe ourselves the same compassion?

Just by accepting ourselves, we make a big change in our lives. We give ourselves credit, and we become a little more humble at the same time. Who are we, after all, to judge ourselves?

Today let me accept myself just as I am.

*There's one thing for which you
can be thankful—only you and
God have all the facts about
yourself.*

Dub Nance

We must become dependent on creating
balance in our lives. We have addictive personalities which means we will always be
vulnerable to switching addictions.

Living a balanced life will help to prevent
switching addictions or going back to our old
addiction. If we eat some, sleep some, exercise some, socialize, attend meetings, read,
work, meditate, and finish our education we
can become well-rounded individuals.

In fact, we will have begun to create a
balance in our lives, and to have good feelings
about that balance and our ability, with help,
to keep it.

*Today let me try to do several things that are
important for healthy living.*

November 7

Grief melts away
Like snow in May,
As if there were no such cold
thing.

George Herbert

It will get better. Whatever hurts us today will be gone another day. It may leave a scar on our hearts, but the suffering will diminish. That powerful, intense pain we feel when we're hurt never lasts forever even though we think it will.

If we lose something important to us, we feel bad and that's okay. But we need to believe that the feelings can and do get better. If we doubt this, all we have to do is look around us and see all the sober people with smiles on their faces, and remember that each and every one of them felt despair at some point and they've lived through it. Things did get better.

Today let me believe that it will get better.

*I am a kind of paranoiac in
reverse. I suspect people of
plotting to make me happy.*

J. D. Sallinger

As addicts, we've spent so much time running toward the things that will hurt us and running away from happiness that we have much unlearning to do. If someone says something kind to us, if someone invites us to a party—these are nice things. These are not things to run away from.

People with addictions become addicted to wh 's familiar, even if that means misery. So to find happiness we have to learn to walk toward it, not away from it.

We can't walk away from happiness today because we've already experienced the bad and we know it's awful. No matter how strange and unfamiliar this happiness feels, we owe it to ourselves to give it a try.

Today help me stay in the happiness.

November 9

I was going to buy a copy of The Power of Positive Thinking, *and then I thought: What the hell good would that do?*

Ronnie Shakes

If we ask someone to a dance and get turned down, we can feel sorry for ourselves or sorry for the other person for losing out on a date with us.

Attitudes can make or break us. A good way to see how positive or negative our attitudes are is to do an attitude check. Whenever we feel down or sorry for ourselves, we ask, "Is there another attitude I can adopt instead?" If there is, then we try to change our negative talk into positive talk. When we go through life with positive attitudes we know lots of miracles will happen.

Today let me remember to check my attitude and keep it positive.

*He who would be serene and pure
needs but one thing, detachment.*

Meister Eckhart

If someone asked to know what recovery was all about in 25 words or less, the Serenity Prayer would probably be the best explanation. We need to accept things like our addiction, our feelings, our past, our limitations, and our inability to change another person. We must be courageous enough to change things that are under our control, like our behavior, our recovery, and our level of self-esteem. And, of course, we have to learn to tell the difference between what we need to accept and what we need to change.

Gladly, the whole process begins with the word *God.* Isn't that a relief? It is God as we understand Him Who takes our hand as we accept the challenges and become sober.

Today help me remember and live by the Serenity Prayer.

*Love doesn't make the world go
'round. Love is what makes the
ride worthwhile.*

Franklin P. Jones

If two people get into a rowboat and try to go somewhere with no oars, they won't make any progress and will probably get sunburned to boot. If only one of them has an oar, they will simply spend the day going in circles. But if both people have oars and the skill to use them, they will reach their destination.

Love is like that too. Both people in a relationship have to be healthy, happy, sober, and willing to grow if the relationship is to be a happy, healthy, productive one.

We are getting better every day. As we grow healthy, we will attract healthy people to us. We can be assured that if we tend to our recovery, healthy love will surely follow.

Today help me remember that a relationship is only as healthy as the people entering into it.

*You don't get to choose how you're
going to die, or when. You can
only decide how you're going to
live now!*

Joan Baez

When we bargain with our recovery, we
are sure to come up empty. If we decide that
we don't need our program, but that our faith
in God alone will keep us sober, we are taking
a great risk. God has given us the tools of
recovery. What else do we expect? It's like the
man drowning who turns down rescue attempts because the Lord will save him. He
drowns, never understanding that the Lord
did try to save him through human rescuers.

We are not alone today because our Higher
Power has given us support in the form of our
fellowship. When we use this support, we are
also exercising our faith in God.

*Today let me see the tools of my rescue that a
loving God has provided me, and use them.*

Good luck is a lazy man's estimate of a worker's success.

Anonymous

If we keep procrastinating instead of getting things done when we should, we might think it's because we're lazy. But laziness is not by itself the problem. Laziness is usually a symptom. It's a symptom of depression or anger or impending relapse. It's a clue that tells us something's wrong.

By referring to ourselves as lazy, we are simply using an excuse to justify our behavior. It's easier to throw up our arms in helplessness and say we're lazy than to do a few simple things to get better. Things like taking our inventory or having a one-to-one talk with a trusted recovering friend or just getting enough rest and nutrition will reward us by raising our energy level.

Today help me to use the tools of recovery to overcome my laziness.

*All family members are out of
touch with their power to gener-
ate good feelings for themselves.*

Sharon Wagscheider

We have spent so much of our lives switching roles and pretending that we wonder who
the real person is inside. We are finding that
trying to hide our pain isn't working anymore.
Some days it feels like we will split in half and
all of our pain and tears will come pouring out.
We wonder sometimes if our friends would
like us if they knew our secrets.

Taking the chance to be our real selves is
worth the scared feelings that might come
with it. Once we know who we are we can
learn to like ourselves. And when we like and
accept ourselves, we no longer have to harbor
shameful secrets and pain. Our lives become
real and joyful when we begin to see we are
acceptable to others.

Today let me let someone see the real me.

*Admitting error clears the score
And proves you wiser than before.*

Arthur Guiterman

Even if they don't say so, our brothers and sisters have been affected by our using. Maybe they had to witness scenes, maybe they had to go out looking for us, maybe we simply took all our parents' attention away. They were affected somehow.

We can make amends to them, if we try. Just telling them we realize they were hurt can help a lot. They may feel they got lost in the shuffle. By telling them we know they were hurt, we can start to make contact with them once again.

Recognizing that they've been affected can bring us closer to a healthy relationship as a family. Learning to listen to our family members is something we can do right now.

Today let me be open to an honest relationship with my siblings.

*It is only well with me when I
have a chisel in my hands.*

Michelangelo

How can we know what we are good at?
What are the talents and gifts that excite us?
What do we do really well? There is a certain
happy feeling of rightness in the pit of the
stomach when we're doing something that's
right for us. Being sober means that we have
a clean connection with our feelings. We now
have the ability to discover what makes us
happy.

The greatest percentage of our time on
earth will be spent working, and we deserve
to wake up happy and anticipating what's in
store for us each day. There is nothing more
pleasing than a person who loves his or her
work, a person who embraces the day feeling
happy and fulfilled.

*Today let me trust myself to explore and de-
velop my own special talent.*

November 17

*There is not a soul who does not
have to beg alms of another,
either a smile, a handshake, or a
fond eye.*

Edward Dahlberg

When we fail at something, it often forces us to accept the guidance and comfort of others. Sometimes we don't seem to have a choice, we have to rely on others. Perhaps God is telling us that we need to learn how to sit back and let others help us. In our recovery program, we are learning that it's healthy to rely on others sometimes.

When we decide to turn our will and our lives over to the care of God, we need to remember that God works through others, and when we fail or stumble, our Higher Power is there for us among our friends and families, and any place where there is love.

Today help me let go of some of the control and let others help me.

*People who fight fire with fire
usually end up with ashes.*

Abigail VanBuren

If someone has hurt us, it's tempting to want to get revenge. It's healthy to make someone responsible for his or her actions, but it's not healthy to plan revenge.

We may have been in the habit of letting people hurt us or take advantage of us. If we take the time and energy needed to plan revenge, we are letting that person control our lives. Now, though, we are developing a healthy sense of our self-worth. We can stop people who hurt us simply by telling them how we feel. By doing this, we refuse to give them any power over us. Today, we are in control of our lives, not others. And our own lives are all we need to feel responsible for. This is one of the freedoms of our recovery.

Today let me refuse to build resentments so I can be free to enjoy my life.

November 19

When you are with a group of people who are really able to be themselves, you will experience a deeply moving sense of well-being.

Stewart Emery

Most of us had no idea who we really were. We were whoever the people around us wanted us to be. We had no self. Our self was too sick for us to want to look at it.

Our recovery is changing the way we look at ourselves. Every day that goes by, we get a little closer to the self we didn't know. Now we have friends who really want to get to know the real us.

We can get excited now about meeting that person who has been buried for so long. We can open up to the people around us and know we can safely show them who we really are.

Today let me chip another layer away and get to know myself better.

Personally, I would sooner have written Alice in Wonderland *than the whole* Encyclopaedia Britannica.

Stephen Leacock

We are all creative in some way. We have been especially creative with the stories we concocted to tell our parents, employers, teachers, or the police to hide our addiction.

Now it's important for us to channel those creative talents into activities that help us grow. We may start playing guitar again or writing music. Perhaps we have talent as a creative and resourceful mechanic.

The goal is to simply create. We have a life now that is open to new things, that allows us to create things: stories, posters, music, or anything that calls upon our ability to develop something that did not exist before.

Today let me begin to create for the pleasure of discovering something new in me.

November 21

*As we advance in life, we learn
the limits of our abilities.*

James Froude

Everything has a price—the good and the bad. Our job is to balance the budget and make sure we don't pay so much that we become emotionally bankrupt. If we're in a rotten relationship, we need to examine the price we're willing to pay to stay in it. If the cost is too high, it's time to get out. If we have unfinished business from the past that needs to be addressed, then with the help of our friends, we can face these problems and solve them.

We no longer have to be pushed along by events. Now we can face our lives and take control. The price we pay is hard work. The reward is freedom.

Today I will weigh the price and rewards of my decisions.

*Peace is something you have or do
not have. If you are yourself at
peace, then there is at least some
peace in the world.*

Thomas Merton

Some people and situations are enough to
make even the most peaceful souls overreact.
Someone might say something that angers
us, or something breaks down just when we
need it most.

Saying, "I am at peace," over and over
again helps fill us with the stillness. We are
at peace with ourselves when we take the
time to be still, to listen to our emotions rather
than simply reacting to them.

We can allow our peaceful nature, the
core of serenity that lies within all of us, to
surface. When we learn this and practice it,
we are living life fully in the present, and
allowing peace its place in our lives.

Today let me feel my inner peace.

*If you always do what you've
always done, you'll always get
what you've always gotten.*

Dr. Jessie Potter

Repeating the same behaviors over and
over, and expecting different results doesn't
make sense. If we keep finding ourselves up
against blank walls, we need to find out why.

Part of us learns to like our old ruts. They
don't seem to get us anywhere but they are
familiar. Sometimes only by getting sick and
tired of being sick and tired can we begin the
process of making positive changes.

When we look at our behaviors, we can
pick and choose the ones to keep. Now we can
work, with the help of our friends and our
Higher Power, to change the behaviors that
cause us problems. Then we'll get what we
never thought possible—happiness.

*Today let me risk letting go of one old negative
habit.*

*That which is striking and
beautiful is not always good, but
that which is good is always
beautiful.*

Ninon De L' Enclos

We all want to be attractive. There's nothing wrong with wanting to look our best as long as we keep it in perspective. If we refuse to go out with good friends because we don't think we look good, we are losing perspective. If we spend a whole night out worrying about whether or not we look good, we are giving up our fun.

The true beauty of a person lies within. It comes from how we treat ourselves and others. It shows in our laughter and our tears. Beauty is a personality trait more than a physical condition, and we are growing in it every day of our recovery.

Today let me see beneath my surface to the beauty within.

*Life sure is easy on a raft, ain't it
Huck?*

Tom Sawyer

Addiction was like an artificial relaxation method that couldn't be trusted. We never knew when that good feeling would turn against us. Addiction with all its frenzied ups and downs is really the opposite of relaxation.

Relaxation is learning how to have fun. It means learning new natural ways to be friendly and kind to our bodies and spirits. We may find it hard to relax at first. We may actually dread quiet, peaceful times. We aren't used to being alone with free time and ourselves.

Our bodies, minds, and spirits need to learn to relax. Now we have the time and the desire to kick back and enjoy the world. All we need to do is be open to new good feelings.

Today let me do one relaxing thing for myself.

*Many individuals have, like
uncut diamonds, shining qualities beneath a rough exterior.*

Juvenal

We all develop at a different pace. It takes
some people a long time to grow into their
gifts and talents. There is a special light deep
within every person. This light is like no
other in the world. It continues to flicker even
when we lose sight of its brightness.

Our light will guide us on the roads of life
that we need to travel. The important thing
is to keep moving and searching. If we never
give up, we will find new and exciting things
about ourselves every day. Gifts and talents
never diminish. They grow strong when we
use them. Now we can look for and appreciate
all of our talents and qualities. All we have to
do to begin is to exercise them in some small
way today.

Today I will believe in my special qualities.

November 27

*Pessimist: One who, when he has
the choice of two evils, chooses
both.*

Oscar Wilde

We need to make budgets and plans for
our futures. Most of us think in ways that are
harmful to our sobriety or our happiness. We
become more concerned with future maybes
than what's happening right now. This is
called "projection."

When we plan, we look at our choices and
decide on the best course for us. Then we take
positive action to make the plan work. When
we project, we spend all of our time worrying
about what the future holds for us.

We don't have to project any more. Today
we can make reasonable plans for our future
based on what we know is best for us. Then we
can look forward to a bright tomorrow.

*Today let me make reasonable plans instead
of fearful projections.*

*A talent is formed in stillness, a
character in the world's torrent.*

Johann von Goethe

Most of us will come across a teacher or
boss we dislike, and the key is to be patient. If
there is no way out of the situation, and we
have already tried talking to the person, we'll
just have to endure. It will pass. This person
won't follow us home and become a perma-
nent fixture in our personal lives.

It might be tempting to talk back or give
sarcastic looks, but those are behaviors that
will only land us up a creek, and we've been
there before. Thankfully, this is a situation
that gets better all by itself as long as we don't
interfere. By being patient, we grow in maturity and develop character. We are learning to
put our intelligence before impulse and we
are teaching those who watch our actions.

*Today let me remember that "This too shall
pass."*

November 29

The world has nothing to bestow;
From our own selves our joys
must flow. . . .

Nathaniel Cotton

For many of us, exercise is just what we do to have a good figure or physique. But that's just the beginning. The best reasons to exercise involve our attitudes. When we exercise, our bodies release endorphins, our brain's natural pain killers, and they are soothing to our feelings of stress and strain. When we exercise we carry more oxygen to the blood and that adds to our feelings of well-being. Exercise is like food to our muscles. It also keeps us feeling limber and flexible. Exercise is good for our complexions and our digestion. It clears our minds, like raising the blinds in a dark room and letting the sun pour in.

Today let me add some exercise to my life. This I'll do in moderation so I don't burn out.

You can't roller skate in a buffalo herd.

Roger Miller

There's a time and a place for everything. When something makes us angry, the time to express that anger is right then, in the present, and the way to do it is directly: we say, "That makes me angry." If we stuff our anger, we end up carrying it around, and it gets hard to carry. It begins to hurt. Often, when this happens, the pent-up anger comes flying out at someone who doesn't deserve it.

Recovery teaches us to take care of things that need taking care of as soon as possible. This way, we don't end up carrying the past around with us. There is a time to forgive ourselves and others. This is growing up, living in the present, and being the best we can be.

Today help me act on my feelings at the right time and in the right place—the present.

December 1

*Most of us are umpires at heart;
we like to call balls and strikes on
somebody else.*

Leo Aikman

When we stop waiting for others to see the errors of their ways and look at ourselves honestly, we begin to feel strong. If we see everybody else's mistakes and don't accept responsibility for our own, we feel weak because nothing gets better.

But when we decide to accept responsibility for our behavior, we have the power to change, we have choices, we have a say-so in our happiness. Having acceptance sounds like we're giving up, but that's not true. What acceptance really means is power. Once we accept who we are and what we are responsible for, we can change. Only when we accept ourselves, can we begin to love ourselves.

Today let me feel the power of acceptance.

*Resolve to thyself; and know that
he who finds himself, loses his
misery.*

Matthew Arnold

Sometimes we do things that hurt ourselves. We don't need anyone else to tell us how we messed up, we are our own worst critics. Explosive anger is like a masked robber that can steal our real feelings.

We can change this negative behavior. We can make a decision to take off our angry masks and let the hurt little boys and girls inside show their real faces. Hurt, fear, and shame are usually hiding under our anger.

Today we can choose to change our out-of-control behaviors. We can take a few deep breaths, take a moment to think, and ask ourselves what it is we are feeling deep down.

Today let me recognize my true feelings.

December 3

The best rule of friendship is to keep your heart a little softer than your head.

Laurence J. Peter

A good friend is a priceless treasure. We feel happy when we are going to meet a good friend and talk. We are learning to value the closeness that the safety of friendship brings.

We now have a few good friends and are practicing being a friend in return. We don't set ourselves up as judges who have all the answers. We work hard at letting our friends know that we accept them exactly as they are. When we put this effort into friendship we get wonderful rewards. We actually feel happy when good things happen to those we care about. We will never be alone because we have friends.

Today let me be a friend to my friends.

How sickness enlarges the dimensions of man's self to himself.

Charles Lamb

It's easy to pity ourselves when we are afflicted with a lifelong disease like addiction. But there is another side to it, a bright side. All we need to do is remind ourselves that if it weren't for our addiction, we wouldn't be recovering. We wouldn't have the friends we have now who love us for ourselves, not for what we can do for them.

We also wouldn't know ourselves as well as we do now. We have worked at knowing and accepting our strengths and weakenesses. We have a relationship with a Higher Power, Who, we know now, has always been there for us. We are growing, and now we have the tools we didn't have before—tools with which to become healthy, loving human beings.

Today let me celebrate something new I've discovered in myself.

December 5

*I woke up Sunday morning with
no way to hold my head that
didn't hurt.*

Kris Kristofferson

Euphoric recall is a strange condition that can affect our recovery. Time seems to dull the pain of our using days and after a while it is possible to start believing that things really weren't so bad. We are on slippery ice when this happens.

Honesty in recovery demands that we stay close to the old hurt. We need to remember our last drunk and know that it would be different this time. It would be worse.

But we are not alone. We have people in our lives today who know how we feel and can help us remember how it really was. More importantly they can help us realize how good our lives are now.

Today let me remember how much better my life is now.

*Who is a holy person? One who is
aware of others' suffering.*

Kabir

We have suffered at the hands of our
addiction. We have lost time, money, friends,
jobs, perhaps even the love and trust of our
closest loved ones. Some of these things we
may never get back. We have been lucky
enough not to have lost life itself. And when
we go to meetings, we find ourselves among
others who have suffered as we have. When
we offer support to our fellows in recovery, we
are giving the precious gift of acceptance, and
in this act, both the giver and the receiver are
no longer alone.

Now we have a way to recognize the
suffering in others because we have stopped
denying it in ourselves. The freedom and
grace in this is enough to fuel another day of
sobriety. What more can we ask?

Today let me offer help to another in need.

December 7

Every individual has a place to fill in the world and is important in some respect, whether he chooses to be so or not.

Nathaniel Hawthorne

Small acts rather than big splashes build our self-esteem. A kind remark to a friend, holding the door for someone—these small things create a strong self-esteem. Most of us think we have to do something awesome to feel like a worthwhile person.

Very few of us make big splashes in life. It's the small, everyday efforts that teach us to like ourselves, respect ourselves, and be proud. Even a marathon runner has to start with short distances before going all the way. Self-esteem is necessary for happiness. It begins with doing some small thing every day that makes us proud.

Today let me do one thing, however small, that makes me proud.

A stumble may prevent a fall

Thomas Fuller

We've all heard the saying, "Pride goeth before a fall." When we get too sure of ourselves, when we stop being careful, that's when we're in danger. In recovery, this could be a life-saving thing to remember. It's easy to feel down when we make mistakes. Often we're tempted to feel that the mistake means we're really getting nowhere at all—that we were just fooling ourselves.

But our Higher Power is watching over us. We get just what we need, not always what we want. So a small stumble now may be an important message to keep our eyes open so we don't suffer a big fall later on. A small stumble is a tool for success because, if we are willing to learn from it, it guides us on a better way.

Today let me be grateful for my mistakes, which help me learn.

December 9

*When people are bored, it is
primarily with their own selves.*

Eric Hoffer

We are not the center of the universe, and
we have been given many hard lessons on
this. Yet sometimes we still expect to be
entertained by life, without having to put any
effort into it. Sometimes we have days where
we feel bored, and boredom can lead to temp-
tations to drink or to get high again.

But we are the entertainers in our life,
and we are discovering many new ways to
have fun. We find pleasure now in simple
things like going for a walk or reading a
book—things our active addiction kept us
from enjoying. When we feel bored, it may be
a reminder from our Higher Power that we
can go out today and discover yet another new
thing to do. And so we grow.

*Today let me enjoy something I had forgotten
could be fun.*

May you live all the days of your life.

Jonathan Swift

Someone once said, "Bring the body and the mind will follow." They were talking about going to meetings, but it seems that saying is true for lots of other things, like job-hunting, exercising, and homework. Today we can begin to practice that saying and watch how true it really is. When we don't feel "in the mood," our bodies can go through the motions anyway. The mind will always follow.

Today we're in control and can fight with the impulse to skip hard work or a meeting. We can take care of the things that will enrich our lives, and ignore the urge to be lazy. Today, we can "bring the body" knowing that, in time, our minds will follow.

Today let me begin to actively lead my life.

December 11

You may break your heart, but men will still go on as before.

Marcus Aurelius

Have we been waiting for someone else to change so we can feel better? Have we been angry because others won't do what we want? This kind of behavior probably isn't new to us. When we were actively addicted, we wanted everyone to change but us. Now we have changed. Whether others do is up to them, just as our changes are up to us.

It may break our heart to see someone we care for living a self-destructive life. But we can live only our own lives. When we accept this, it is easier to live the way our Higher Power has in mind for us. When we do what we need to do for ourselves, our lives will become full in ways we can't know in advance, and our hearts will be strong and unbroken.

Today help me to let go of trying to get others to do what I want.

If the world seems cold to you,
kindle fires to warm it!

Lucy Larcom

Sometimes doing the healthy thing can seem lonely. When we were using, we had many people in our lives we called friends. Often though, the only thing we had in common with these friends was our using. When we stopped using, they stopped being friends.

In the beginning it was easy to feel that we would never have friends again. We know now that this isn't true. Little by little, we are learning to open up to new people. We are making new friends. Now we can see, through our new and growing ability to love and be a friend, how important our sobriety is. Our recovery is what makes our friendships possible.

Today let me remember there are new friends just waiting to meet me.

December 13

Truth is the daughter of time.

Anonymous

When we were drinking or using, sometimes we loved the feeling we had when we were high. Our fear fell away. We could stand in a room and not want to rush for a corner or the door. We felt all-powerful or attractive. And when we crashed later, no matter how bad we felt, we still believed that our drug of choice could take us back to that place.

In recovery our truths and beliefs change. So do our feelings. Now we can have feelings lined with love and serenity instead of lies, feelings that little by little teach us the exact words to say whenever we need to say them, feelings that we can share.

Today help me realize one truth about my past and help me let go of it.

*Time makes more converts than
reason.*

Tom Paine

We remember well how uncontrollable
our own lives were when we were in the grips
of active addiction. In order to begin recovery,
we had to admit we were powerless. Now, to
stay and grow in recovery, we have to remind
ourselves we are powerless. We are not only
powerless over our drug of choice, we are also
powerless over other people. We can't force
others to change, no matter how wrong they
seem. The sooner we admit this to ourselves,
the sooner we will begin to know peace. We
can patiently let others learn their own lessons their own way, the way we learned ours.
For each of us, the timing is different. We can
learn to accept, with the help of our Higher
Power, and to live with the differences.

*Today help me pay attention to my own timing
for change, and to let go of others.*

December 15

*Life is a great bundle of little
things.*

Oliver Wendell Holmes

Often when others ask us what's going on
we say, "Oh, nothing." Perhaps we say this
because we don't want to talk to that person
at all, or because we're a little lazy that day.
In fact, there is always something going on.
As long as we are alive, things are happening
in our lives—most of them little things.

When we are truly living in the present,
we are open to all sorts of things. We are
aware of life going on around us as well as
being aware of our own concerns. Living in
the present means paying attention to the
small things going on right now. In living this
way we expand our lives, increase the rich-
ness of our present, and make ourselves more
available to the world around us.

*Today let me be aware of life around me, and
thank my Higher Power for my part in it.*

*There are two types of people in
this world: Those who come into
a room and say, "Well, here I
am!" and those who say, "Ah,
there you are!"*

Anonymous

Which type of person will we choose to be
today? Will we focus on ourselves or others?
The days we find we enjoy life the most are the
days during which we focus on reaching out to
others.

Once, we didn't trust ourselves to be good
friends to others or to ourselves, either. Today
it feels terrific to care about our friends. We
value our growing ability to really care about
the other person. We want to be there for our
friends. When we sit across the table from
someone and share a cup of coffee, we enjoy
feeling connected. We're not alone any more.

*Today let me be the person who says, "Ah,
there you are!"*

December 17

*He would like to start from
scratch. Where is scratch?*

Elias Canetti

We have begun our lives all over again,
haven't we? We have given up old behaviors
that used to rule us, and with them we have
given up many friends, activities, and places.
Why then do we still have so many of the old
problems, like anger, self-hate, fear, shyness,
or lack of confidence?

The truth is, most people wrestle with
these problems at one time or another. We
start from scratch when we ask for help.
When we admit we need help, we are ready to
begin again. There's nothing wrong with
admitting we're wrong. When we see that
we're able to start over, we free ourselves to
try many more things we've never tried before—as though we're beginning a new life.

*Today let me be willing to start over if things
don't go right.*

*What is grace? I know until you
ask me; when you ask me, I do
not know.*

Saint Augustine

Many of us thought there was no help for
us. The idea that we were being guided and
helped by a Higher Power was foreign to us.

We not only didn't know about the Higher
Power, we fought the idea when we were told.
But, by listening to those around us, we started
to understand. Now we can see all the times
in our lives when we shouldn't have lived;
times when we took risks that did kill the
bodies and souls of others.

It is grace that brought us through dark,
lonely nights, and grace that finally brought
us to recovery. We can be thankful today for
the grace to be a real part of our own lives and
the lives of those around us.

*Today let me remember that, "There, but for
the grace of God, go I."*

December 19

The best way out is always
through.

Robert Frost

Sometimes we're so afraid of something that we avoid it as completely as we can. It may be that we need to confront someone we care about, or ask for a raise. By avoiding it, we give that thing power it would not have on its own. We let it dominate us.

There is very little in our lives which will go away on its own. Surprisingly, though, when we turn around and face things directly, we find they are not so hard to do after all.

Most people do this from time to time. Maybe we have more fears than other people, but we also have a lot of courage. Facing up to addiction and admitting we are powerless is no small feat. It takes courage. If we have courage to admit powerlessness, we have courage to do much more.

Today help me face one thing I have feared.

Silence is essential to every happy conversation. But not too much silence.

Myles Connolly

We are happily learning about the art of friendship. We view it as a give and take, talk and listen, experience. When we were using we demanded center stage. We thought our troubles were the most important things in the world. We expected our friends to do all the listening. We gravitated toward those people who were caretakers and fixers. We thrived on the silence of others.

Now we're learning to fill our own needs, and we can give the gift of silence to our friends. We can listen.

Today we have learned to trust ourselves enough to risk being a friend to others. We know now that friends listen as well as talk.

Today let me learn to share true friendship.

December 21

It is better to ask some of the questions than to know all of the answers.

James Thurber

Today we are grateful that we don't have to have all the answers. We used to pretend that we knew more than we really did. We felt we had to have an answer to almost everything. We are learning to take a step back from center stage. We can feel comfortable being honest and saying, "I don't know." We feel good about this progress in our recovery.

Today we enjoy being ourselves—not so perfect people who are continuing to learn. We are a lot less afraid to get up in the mornings these days. Now we accept our limitations and want to continue to have the courage to be open to learning.

Today let me have more questions than answers.

*A great deal of intelligence can be
invested in ignorance when the
need for illusion is deep.*

Saul Bellow

When we're having thoughts like, "I'm different than everyone else at meetings," or "I'm not lying, I'm just leaving out certain facts," or "I can handle going to a using party," we know we're using stinking thinking.

The way we know this is how we feel in our guts. Somewhere inside of us we're uncomfortable and a voice is crying out, "Hey you! You're making an old mistake." If we ignore this little voice by pushing it out of the way as we head for disaster, we will surely regret it later. Today we want to keep an ear tuned for the little voice that warns us of stinking thinking. We want to knock down the stinking thinking and clear the way to travel the road of freedom and joy.

Today let me keep my mind open and free.

December 23

*You can't hold a man down
without staying down with him.*

Booker T. Washington

This is not our old life. In our old life, we got angry and stayed angry, holding resentments against people who often had no idea we were angry at them. Now we can choose to express our feelings immediately when we are angry. We can free ourselves from anger.

This new life is one we choose each day. We choose not to drink or get high, and we choose not to abuse ourselves with anger and blame. Old anger hurts no one but ourselves. It robs us of our energy and distracts us from the good things life has to offer.

By expressing our anger right away and then forgiving as soon as we can, we free ourselves from old prisons and grow in our freedom and our new joy.

Today let me express my negative feelings and let go of them.

*We could choose to see the world
through the window of love rather
than through the window of fear.*

Dr. Gerald Jampolsky

What are we afraid of? We all fail once in a while. We may suffer injuries no matter how careful we are. This doesn't mean we must hide from life. On the contrary, it means we have just what it takes to live bravely—fear. If we had no fear, we wouldn't need bravery. Yet we have already done one of the bravest things a person can do: we have given up our drug of choice. We have admitted our powerlessness and asked for help. We are turning our lives over to our Higher Power

When we begin to see that there are rich rewards out there for us, we can begin to see that love lives inside us right alongside our fear. We have the choice of which we pay attention to, and which we act on.

Today help me act out of love instead of fear.

December 25

*When we refuse to forgive our-
selves, we participate in a form of
negative grandiosity.*

Mary Remarque

It's easy to blame ourselves for all the
suffering we've had. It's easy to feel worthless
and hopeless. But we no longer need to do
this. We're living a new life now, a healing,
growing life.

Our Higher Power is all-forgiving. Who
are we to keep judging ourselves so harshly?
Is it because we know more than God?

We can't control others. We can't control
our addiction. And we can't change the past.
We have no right to refuse to forgive ourselves. Hard as it is to forgive ourselves, this
is our job, and our challenge. When we find it,
we open a door to glittering freedom—freedom from fear, from self-hate, from the past.

*Today let me accept my human limits, and
forgive at least one thing I've done.*

*It doesn't take a medical genius to
see that procrastinators aren't too
big on success. I suppose you
could say they fear success.*

Stephanie Gulp

"I'll do it tomorrow." We can put things off
until we feel paralyzed by guilt. The more we
delay the worse we feel and the worse we feel
the more we delay. It doesn't seem to help
when we analyze why we procrastinate. The
only cure for putting things off is to take
action.

We know today what needs to be done in
our lives. We don't have to worry about next
week or next year. Now we know that we can
do the next thing that needs doing. When we
finish that, we can go on to the next thing. By
doing one next thing that needs doing, we find
that nothing goes undone and our tomorrows
take care of themselves.

*Today let me do each next thing that needs
doing.*

December 27

*Think of all the beauty still left
around you and be happy.*

Anne Frank

What do we have now that we didn't have when we were using? This is a question we can ask ourselves a lot. It's counting our blessings and keeping things in perspective.

Gratitude is a word that we had little use for when we were actively addicted. We didn't think we had anything to be grateful for. We were unhappy and restless.

Now we can look around and see all the things we can be grateful for. Most of these will be small things—waking up feeling good in the morning or having nothing to hide. Progress and gratitude go together. The more grateful we become, the more progress we've made.

Today let me be grateful for my progress and rejoice in it!

To rejoice at another person's joy
is like being in heaven.

Meister Eckhart

What did we used to feel when something good happened to someone else? Maybe envy. Maybe self-pity. Maybe we thought that life wasn't fair, or maybe we hated the person for their good fortune. Why them and not us?

In one way or another, all those feelings served us, protected us, got us through when nothing else could. But now they're pretty much obsolete. They don't feel good and they just don't work.

In recovery we are learning about joy. We are learning that it takes nothing away from us—but adds—to feel joy for another, to rejoice in someone else's happiness. In recovery we find a joy that has to do not with having or not having, but with the courage to be, the courage to be seen, the courage to give.

Today let me feel joy for another's joy.

December 29

Weeping may remain for a night, but rejoicing comes in the morning.

Psalms 30:5

Sadness is not necessarily something to be gotten rid of. Sadness is a normal human emotion. If a relationship ends before we're ready, if we get passed over for a job we applied for, it would be odd not to feel some sadness. The problem comes when we blow sadness out of proportion.

Once, every sadness was a major tragedy for us. We had no way of coping with even small upsets. Now we do. We can feel sad today and know that the sadness will pass. We know now that sadness, like joy, is a part of everyone's life. We can look at our emotions honestly and learn to control them   Our emotions no longer control us.

Today let me remember that whatever is making me sad will pass.

*The years teach us much which
the days never knew.*

Ralph Waldo Emerson

We don't need to know everything today, and so we don't. We don't know why some people act the way they do, or why we are addicts when others aren't. All we need to know today is what to do to preserve sobriety for this day. This means doing the small things we need to do right now.

We live life from moment to moment, and we can be grateful for that. There is nothing too hard to do for this moment only. We are clean and sober this moment, and so we are growing. As we live our day fully today, we will find no part of it bigger than the moment it occupies.

Today let me live life the best I can by staying in the present.

December 31

*I'm looking through you. You're
not the same.*

Paul McCartney

Now that we have been sober for a time,
our old life may begin to look a little different
to us. Perhaps we have run into some of our
old friends and we are surprised by how
different we see them now. Maybe we find
ourselves thinking about the good time we
used to have with them, and so they seem
more fun than they actually were. Or we see
their preoccupation with getting high, and so
their lives seem limited to us now.

Whichever way we see them, it's not the
same. Old times never come again. What we
have now is a new life, a new way of seeing
ourselves and our friends, and we are making
new friends who really care about us and our
sobriety. We will never be alone again as long
as we stick to the program.

Today help me see the goodness in my new life.